For Brent

A friend may well be reckoned the masterpiece
of nature. - Ralph Waldo Emerson

King of the Blue

For those who have a passion for the ocean, and for all those creatures who live their lives beneath the waves, the author of 'King of the Blue' will submerge the reader beneath the sea and away from the reassuring heat of the sun. Plunging into the cool, pitch blackness of a moonless ocean, the strong taste of salt will invade your every pore, as your senses blur and your ears echo to an unmistakable sound; a sound that makes the hairs upon the back of your neck stand on end!

Where you sense no life, there hides a multitude.
Where you see no eyes, eyes are upon you.
Where you sense no danger, there danger lurks!

Book 1.

"Turning the Tide."

1.
A fresh tide. A new life.

Safely cocooned within his mother's womb, the calf felt the walls of his small world begin to flex and to strain, as his mother's muscles rippled with her natural urge to deliver her offspring. Tiring of trying to fight the mounting pressure as his mother continued to push, the calf, feeling cramped and fighting the building pressure, struggled to understand what was happening to him. Hearing the change in strength and tone of the constant pinging and clicking sounds that came from the world outside, the yet to be delivered calf waited, his small heart pounding, for his mother's last great effort.

Sensing that the time had finally arrived for him to leave the safety and security of his tiny sea, within a sea, that he had called home for so long, and with a mind filled with more questions than there were answers, he felt his mother's tissue roll with the strength of a wave as she forcefully delivered her long-awaited baby from her body.

The chill touch of a spring sea on his skin shocked the new arrival in a way that left his senses reeling to the tastes and sounds of his new environment. Wriggling his tail he swam close to his mother and the safety of her reassuring form. This was not what the newborn had expected at all. This was a very different feeling from the warmth he had left inside the safety and security of his mother's womb. The unexpected chill of the cool water made his skin tingle, as in one moment his senses changed to examine a new and much more frightening sensation. Feeling his body burst through the surface in a small cloud of foam and spray, he took heed of an inner message which told him to breathe.

Drawing in his first breath he gasped at the coolness of the fresh sea air as it tickled his untested lungs. The many exciting scents and tastes that his small breathing hole drew in, were as frightening and confusing to him as anything he had yet known. He felt the shock of this new feeling, crisp and sharp, as the thrilling sensation sent a tingling throughout the length of his body. Feeling a slight bump against his flank, he sensed his mother's presence swimming close at his side. Swimming close to her side he found a feeling of safety at her reassuring touch on his skin, as she caressed her newborn son lovingly with the tip of her smooth snout.

With his ears echoing to his mother's reassuring clicks and pings, the calf heard his mother's tone for the very first time.

'I see you, small one,' toned his mother, Sorryl. 'Come, swim close to me and breathe as you need to.' Relaxing in the sea, the newborn floated with the aid of his mother swimming on one side, and the great bulk of Nee-Lah, his mother's older companion, swimming on the other. With their help he began to learn the art of diving and surfacing. Exhaling the old air, and breathing in the sharp, clean air that his small body required to fuel his as yet untried muscles. Staring wide-eyed, he studied the large presence swimming at his side.

Feeling the strong connection to his mother, he recognized her calming tones from his time spent growing in her womb. With her image stamped firmly in his mind, the newly arrived calf turned his attention to the elderly Nee-Lah, who swam protectively on his other flank, as his mother and Nee-Lah guided him gently with their bodies. He could feel their strength, as he felt himself rising in the sea, as they carefully lifted him to the surface to enable him to breathe, before guiding him back down into the all-embracing depths of his undersea home. Swimming close to his mother, there was one thing that the calf knew for sure, and that was that he was feeling hungry. Very hungry!

Sensing a tiny rumbling coming from her new charge, the elderly Nee-Lah guided him gently down and beneath his mother, to where his still immature senses quickly located the source of his mother's milk. Attaching himself at his mother's teat, the newborn set to, greedily suckling Sorryl's thick creamy milk. Nee-Lah watched him closely. Sensing the urgency in the newborn's feeding, she proceeded to remove him from the teat with a firm, yet gentle push of her broad snout, guiding him back upward toward the surface.

Not enjoying this interruption at all, and having grabbed another hesitant breath, he immediately swam back down with a flick of his tail, to hurriedly re-attach himself to the reassuring form of his mother.

'So,' piped an amused Nee-Lah, 'the small one has the appetite of his father. He will not grow strong and large if he does not first remember to breathe!'

Stuck to his mother's belly and sucking for all he was worth, the calf caught a first glimpse of a dark shadow as he felt his ear echo to his father's deep toned greeting. Feeling his skin prickle, the calf watched nervously out of the corner of his eye as his father made his first appearance since his birthing. 'You have done very well, Sorryl, mother of the sea,' boomed Torkahn. 'You have delivered us a fine son to mark the new moon. For this, I thank you.

'I thank you, too, Nee-Lah, for your loyalty and service to Sorryl. Please do not forget that my son has the blood of the Tor-Gah running through his veins. See that he feeds well, for we have many breaths to make, and much distance to cover before we may rest again.'

'I hear your tone, my Tor,' called Nee-Lah, her musical call sounding in the water as she bowed her noble head so that she might avoid the penetrating stare of Torkahn's all-seeing eye.

'Your new son feeds like his father once did. Surely he will drink too much and sink straight to the depths of the blue!' toned Nee-Lah, her teasing echo lost to the brief silence that followed.

'Enough, old mother!' returned Torkahn. 'I will hold you personally responsible should my son turn out to be, too, laden with blubber to ever swim at the head of the Tor-Gah!'

With her smiling eye meeting Torkahn's, the elderly Nee-Lah moved away using lazy strokes of her tail, leaving Torkahn to share this special moment with his mate, as he stared in wonder at the first sight of his newly born son.

With a wink of his eye to Nee-lah, Torkahn swam close to taste and to experience for the very first time, the sweet scent of his newly delivered son.

Nuzzling Sorryl's flank in a demonstration of his love and support for his mate, the powerful Torkahn shared a few guarded tones of his satisfaction at the safe delivery of the newest addition to their aquatic family. In a low and most delicate call, Torkahn gave tone to his first thoughts to his youngest son.

'I see you, son of the Tor-Gah. Mark my scent well, small one, for you are of my blood.'

Dwarfed by the magnificent size of his father, the newborn found that he felt no fear at the sudden appearance of something so large, and so dominating, as a fully grown Orca. Feeling more surprised than afraid, the young calf felt the lingering effects of a strong warmth shared through this first meeting with his awesome father. Sensing that his dominating presence had been noticed by his son, Torkahn swam pleased and relieved at his safe delivery to the blue.

Closing his eyes Torkahn pictured his mate and his new born. This was a morning worth remembering. Returning his attention to the leadership of the pod, his pod, now with yet another small life becoming part of his responsibility, Torkahn sent tone for Nee-Lah, calling for her to swim to him.

Hearing Torkahn's tone calling for her through the water, Nee-Lah could sense Torkahn's great pleasure and relief at the safe arrival of his son. Seeking Torkahn in the dimly lit sea, Nee-Lah marveled at the sheer size and beauty of the now fully mature and powerful Torkahn. She had watched over the passing of many summers' as Torkahn had grown completely unrecognizable from the small 'Torky' she had come to know and love, and at times, to suckle when Torkahn's own mother, the patient and serene Soh-lae-lah, had had more than enough of a young Torkahn's constant demands for more and more of her rich milk. Drawing her mind back to the present, Nee-Lah sent tone in reply to Torkahn.

'I am here, my Tor. Is something wrong?'
Moving through the water at a comfortable pace, Torkahn eyed Nee-Lah, swimming close to the elderly female before sharing his reply.

'Why has the arrival of my son surprised you all so?'
Nee-Lah sensed Torkahn's concern sounding in his tone.

'The tide of chance, oh great, Torkahn. I regret that I cannot control the flow of the tides any more than you can change the course of a current,' Nee-Lah toned in answer to Torkahn's question. Torkahn's ear vibrated as he recognized the familiar and tunefully teasing tone of the elderly Nee-Lah.

'You must learn to have patience, my Tor. The new life for which you have been waiting so long, has arrived. Earlier than I had expected, I admit. He seems strong and all goes well. Even you, great Tor, were early to the blue, and after all, it is your own son who has upset your own carefully laid plans, is it not?'

Moving forward in the sea, Torkahn allowed his body to rise higher in the water as he sent a gust of used air, shot from his blowhole with an ominous hiss, high into the cool morning air.

'Very well, Nee-Lah. I hear your tone and bow to your obvious experience in these most delicate of matters,' he toned. Torkahn enjoyed trading tone with Nee-Lah. After the passing of so many tides, he can come to trust the whale he considered to be his second mother. Nee-Lah was a listener, and most importantly, the elderly Nee-Lah knew how to hold her tone. He could share things with Nee-Lah that he would never think of sharing with any other member of the pod. It was to the faithful Nee-Lah that he now entrusted the care of his newly born son. If he was the head of this family, then surely Nee-Lah was the heart.

Sensing Torkahn's obvious concern and unease, Nee-Lah sought to change the drift of Torkahn's mind.

'What name will you give to this new son of the Tor-Gah?' Meeting Nee-Lah's eye with his own, Torkahn gave tone in answer to her searching question.

'Sorryl has decided upon Torryn,' he replied, giving the name an added ring to it with his tuneful delivery. Nee-Lah eyed Torkahn through an all seeing eye.

'So a dam makes decisions for the mighty Tor?' she teased. As Nee-Lah had come to expect, Torkahn's response was a predictable one for a large bull Orca.

'I hear you, Nee-Lah. Please, do not test me. I have no time to worry of names. I have only the time to worry for us all, and for the life of the pod.' Hearing Torkahn's deep tone of reply Nee-Lah could sense the tiredness sounding in Torkahn's call.

'I hear you, my Tor, and I understand. Your father was the same. Always with an eye on tomorrow's dawn and the flow of the next tide. It is your time Torkahn. Enjoy the gift that the new tide has delivered to us this day,' Nee-Lah encouraged. Moving to place himself closer to Nee-Lah's side, Torkahn placed his head closer to hers, before sharing his whispered tone,

'I thank you, Nee-Lah, for your concern. You are mother to us all.'

Hearing Torkahn's response Nee-Lah toned her farewell, before, with a regal bow of her head, she swam from Torkahn's side to rejoin a slowly swimming and very relieved Sorryl, and the new born son, Torryn.

As she swam, she called to her latest charge. 'Welcome Tor-Rah-Nah, son of Tor.' To Torkahn's ear the name sounded with the gentleness of a small current caressing a rounded stone. The surrounding sea echoed to the gentle tones of the new mother, as she happily clicked and pinged in total admiration of her newborn son. Reluctant to leave the presence of his beautiful mate and his newly arrived son, Torkahn turned in the sea with a heavy tail, to return to his position and to issue fresh orders for the pod. Watching as Torkahn's shadow faded in the sea, Nee-Lah had been very much aware that the time running up to the birthing had been especially hard for Torkahn. Allowing her memory to drift back over countless tides, she recalled the day that the fiercely loyal Torkahn had lost his first mate, the mother to his sons' Rally and Daks, so many moons ago. Torkahn's much loved first mate had died after suffering from an illness that had appeared from out of the deep at a sickening speed, to claim lives at a time when the tight family unit had been least expecting it.

Sensing the hidden depth of Torkahn's sorrow at losing his mate, Nee-Lah had watched over the passing of many tides to see that memory fade, and for the Tor's great pain of loss to lessen within him. Through his mating with the fine tailed, Sorryl, and with Torryn's successful birth, the time was now right for Torkahn to put these feelings behind him, as a fresh tide and a new moon gave them all hope for a future, free from such worry and loss. Nee-Lah knew only too well, that such things and wounds of the heart heal only through the passing of time and tide. With a beautiful new mate swimming at his side, and a fine new son added to his already grown family, Nee-Lah recognized that the tide of change, and the current of good fortune, had at last turned to run in Torkahn's favour.

 Spy-hopping in the sea Torkahn enjoyed the warmth of the sun's rays against his skin. He felt tense. Coiled tight like a sea-snake. He felt wildly elated and found that he had to fight a strong urge to just swim! Nee-Lah was right. It was his time. Sending strength to his tail he swam toward Rally who waited in the sea ahead. Torkahn sent tone to his eldest son.
'You have a new young brother, Rah-leh-lah! He is perfectly formed and swims well!' Surprised to see his father acting in such a way, Rally's ear caught the good news.

News that the entire pod had been so anxiously waiting to hear.

'Take over the lead, Rally,' called Torkahn. 'I will not be too long away.'

Watching his father's form disappear into the gloom of an early morning sea, Rally swam to find his brother Daks. Daks, too, was equally puzzled by their father's behavior.

'Should we not follow?' Daks toned.

'No, Daks. I think father wishes to swim alone. It is his time,' returned Rally.

Driving himself faster and faster through the water with every push of his powerful tail, Torkahn sped through the sea enjoying the feeling of the water caressing every inch of his smooth skin, as he swam over the sand bar at the mouth of the bay, and out into the raw freedom of the open ocean.

With every push of his tail Torkahn felt the worry and strain of the past years falling behind him in his churning wake.

As he continued to gather speed through the water, he took a last hurried breath, before angling his body downward, to dive down into the near inky blackness.

Diving deep, his tail drove him effortlessly through the sea. Checking his dive, he angled his body upward, to swim with all of his strength toward the slight glimmer of light that marked the surface far above him.

Sending every last ounce of strength to his tail, Torkahn felt himself burst from the surface, his entire body pulling itself free from the water, launched by the strength of his thrusting tail!

Feeling the water rushing down his body, streaming in a torrent of foam and spray, Torkahn reached the top of his perfect flight. Feeling himself flying free above the waves, he soon felt the forces of gravity pulling him all too quickly back to the water below. Falling onto his side with an almighty smack, his body returned to the sea, his weight creating a large hole that quickly refilled through a flood of waves and spray, as the sea swallowed him up in a foaming swirl. Enjoying the sheer pleasure of his freedom and his joy at the successful birth of his son, Torkahn felt as if he had the strength and will to swim every ocean which covered the earth!

2.
A first meeting.

Enjoying the first light of the new day as he swam, Torkahn took care to greet each member of his pod as he passed. Swimming toward the sound of early morning chatter, he came upon the younger females who swam under his protection. 'I see you young dams,' he toned, in his most polite manner. 'Never has the blue seen such a fine selection of young maidens.' The two young females, Sey-lah and Soh-nee, mates to his sons' Rally and Daks, each returned Torkahn's greetings in musical unison.

Torkahn's eye fell on the twin forms swimming at their mothers' sides; his two grand-daughters. Their names were Torney and Nayla. Torkahn sent out a series of unusual clicks and pulses that seemed to highly amuse the two younger calves, who twittered in a rather shy manner as they attempted to hide behind the larger bodies of their mothers'.

The third female, known as Sorryl, his Sorryl, was the niece of Nee-Lah. Never had Torkahn been so lost for tone as when he had first set his eye on the graceful form of his fine-tailed mate. He had thought that he would never again find such a treasure of the sea after the loss of his first mate so long ago. Feeling his thoughts drifting, Torkahn forced his mind to return to the present, and to his mate, and to the small form of their hungry new arrival swimming at Sorryl's side.

Keeping a close eye on the appearance of Rally and Daks, Torkahn spotted the younger bull, Kola, who swam hidden from view behind his eldest sons. Torkahn watched with an ever vigilant eye as the small group of males swam far too close to Sorryl, Torryn and the shape of the always watchful Nee-Lah. Before he could send tone, Torkahn felt his ear vibrate to Nee-Lah's sharply delivered warning.

'I see you, Rally, son of Torkahn. You would do well to turn your head and swim away. Surely there are more important things for the son of the Tor to busy himself with?' Hearing Nee-Lah's playful scolding of his eldest son, Torkahn took quick charge.

'I see you, Rah-leh-lah. You will take Kola to seaward and patrol our open flank. You will travel a distance of two hundred breaths and then you will return. Remember to keep your eyes peeled for cold-bloods, Rally. Your new sibling's life depends upon you.'

Taking heed of his father's order, and giving a brief click to Kola, the two Orca thrashed their tails in unison as they reluctantly turned their heads toward the mouth of the bay.

Turning his attention to Daks, Torkahn gave tone to a similar command.

'Hear me, Daks. Leave away from the females and relieve Kona of his duty.'

'I hear you, Tor,' Daks responded in answer to his father's call. Sounding his own farewells to the females, Daks took a deep breath before submerging, as he, too, set off on his long swim to relieve Kona. With their father's tone still ringing in their ears, Rally and Daks met beneath the waves before swimming off together, their tails waving as they jostled each other with powerful, yet playful sideswipes. Kola swam to follow on behind, doing his best to keep his body surfing in Rally's fast moving slipstream. Swimming at speed toward the shifting sandbar that ran across the mouth of the bay, Rally gave Daks a last nudge before angling his body upward to clear the steeply rising bar. The silt and sand being carried along by the last of the outgoing tide race making for a clouded sea. With several powerful downward thrusts of his tail, Daks was soon lost from sight as he swam quickly in the direction of the northern side of the channel, on his way to locate Kona, Kola's often quiet and brooding father who swam on patrol many breaths to the north.

Swimming swiftly through the sea Kola had been enjoying the friendly tussle and rivalry between Rally and Daks. It was at that moment that the more powerful Rally chose to test Kola's own speed and agility. With several powerful tail thrusts, Rally pushed ahead at speed, leaving an unprepared Kola behind in a swirl of sand and debris. Sensing the challenge, Kola added strength to his own tail and powered after Rally, determined to match Rally's speed through the sea. Passing over the high sand-bar and breaking into clear water, Rally, much to his surprise and astonishment found himself swimming nose to nose with a large Mako shark! The shark had, at that exact moment, been considering swimming over the bar and entering the bay, his keen senses having confirmed the source of the enticing blood scent in the sea following Torryn's birth. There was no telling who was the more surprised! Rally and Kola were certainly taken unawares by the sneaking presence of so many cold-bloods, and all swimming so close to the unsuspecting members of the pod! Moving at such a speed through the sea that coming to a full stop was simply out of the question, Rally immediately recognized the sudden danger. Sending a pulse of sonar that bounced back off of the rocks as a warning to Kola, Rally increased his speed further with a sudden flurry of rapid tail thrusts. Keeping a close and steady eye on his target, Rally slammed into the biggest

Mako head-first at considerable speed! This surprise and very aggressive attack knocked the Mako hard, as Rally opened his jaws in an attempt to get a bite onto the sharks exposed back. Rolling under the impact of Rally's terrific blow, the Mako's wide eye caught the blurred image of Rally's flashing teeth! The shark went for the seabed with a flash of his tail, to disappear from sight in the blink of an eye. Appearing just in time to see two Mako going in for a panicked attack on Rally's exposed tail, Kola punched his nose into the pale belly of one of the Mako. Swimming a tight circle and rolling over almost upside down, Rally snapped out, catching the other cold-blood by the tip of its tail! Leaving an excited Rally to wrestle with his new friend, Kola swam to chase off the remainder of the Mako into the depths, before circling back to find Rally still clinging to the tail of his attacker, who by this time, was thrashing about in a desperate attempt to free itself from Rally's vice like grip.

Kola could see that Rally was having a great time! Finally letting go of the Mako's tail, they watched as the shark shot forward at a rapid pace, to disappear in a flash of light to follow the others, lost from sight in the curtained gloom of an overcast sea.

'Should we not give chase, Rally?' Kola toned. Rally turned to eye his younger partner.

'No, Kola. The cold-bloods have learned their lesson today. To chase them would only be a fruitless search. They will have run far and deep,' toned Rally. 'Besides, it would be foolish to spill fresh blood here, right on our own foreshore.'

'Should we not report to the Tor, Rally, surely…?'

'The Tor has more than enough to consider, Kola!' Rally's tone dropped to that of a whisper as he looked Kola directly in his rounded eye.

'Would you trouble the Tor with your confession of our deliberate failure to secure the bay and the entrance?' toned Rally. 'We looked on to watch the birth of my new half- brother like a pair of worried dams. No, Kola, we will not lay the weight of our failure upon the Tor's already heavy burden. This little meeting will stay between the two of us, I think.'

'I hear you, Rally,' toned Kola. The sound of his call revealing his fear of their near failure to protect the pod.

'We were lucky, Kola,' Rally toned quietly. 'But that was fun!' called Rally, in a more cheerful tone. 'Did you see how that one wriggled as I tried to shake some sense into him? I think we have seen the last of that bunch of brutes, Kola, but I shall remember the big one,' toned Rally, his call trailing off to be scattered to the deep.

'I hope you are right, Rally,' returned Kola, his eyes staring out into the hidden and shaded depths of the sea.

Having made his escape the big Mako swam at speed into the darkness of the deeper water, confident that he had again lived to eat another day. With his confidence shaken, he swam wide-eyed and unblinking through the sea, his brief encounter already forgotten as he sought out his scattered companions.

Kola continued to watch and to listen long after the big Mako had made its escape. He swam unsure whether they had done the right thing by their not having reported to the Tor on their violent encounter with so many of the Mako. Like Rally, Kola knew that he would recognize the big Mako the next time they swam across his course. Kola swam with a strong feeling that this would not be the last time that they saw this fish. The light had already started to grow as the sun rose on the eastern horizon. Kola's eye reacted to the change in light which marked the beginning of another day. Kola had recognized that the large Mako had been using the change in light to their advantage, at a time he knew when all the creatures that made their home beneath the sea must take great care to swim with their eyes wide-open.

3.

Where you sense no danger.

Rising up out of a bloodied, foaming sea, the grey head shook from side to side as the shark fed greedily on the luckless carcass of his early morning kill.

As the Mako continued to feed, the sea surrounding him foamed with a crimson stain and the heady scent of death. The ravenous shark felt the envious eyes of many of his kind watching him, as other dark triangles broke the surface some distance from the site of his bloody kill. The feeding shark had long since sensed their looming presence, using his inbuilt sensors which ran the length of his well-muscled body. If these new arrivals were hoping for some small share in his well-won prize, then they would all be disappointed.

The seven deadly hunters swam slowly beneath the surface of the sea. Falling into a loose line, the sharks, their bellies still empty, trailed after their well-fed leader. One by one, each of their triangular dorsal fins disappeared from sight, to be lost beneath the ruffled surface of a still settling sea.

The leading Mako was known to his followers as
Zaar. He was big, measuring four meters long,
from the tip of his scarred and pointed snout, to
the point of his slender tail. His powerful body
weighing in at four hundred kilos. He was like
all of his kind, a living, breathing, eating
machine, and Zaar was hungry!

Moving with a careful stealth through the sea,
Zaar's eye caught the blurred outlines of his
shadows. Zaar swam aware that he was being
followed by others of his own kind.
Though he much preferred to hunt alone, Zaar
knew that extra numbers often made for an
easier kill. He had made it clear to these Mako
using his own brute strength that they should
never swim to interfere with his hunting without
his invitation to do so. Each of his followers
swam in silent respect of Zaar's immense size
and physical strength, each having been
attracted by Zaar's well-deserved and fierce
reputation.
As a group, none of them lacked the courage to
swim in Zaar's wake. Each shark swam aware
that Zaar always managed to find prey that was
both plentiful, and more than likely an easy kill.
Leading his pack, Zaar swam with easy strokes
of his muscular tail. He moved cautiously.
Taking great care to make sure that their
movements were well-hidden by the constant
motion of the broken and silt-churned sea.

Swimming with purpose through the shaded gloom of the overcast dawn, Zaar's sharpened senses detected a presence moving through the disturbed fog of the sea.

Closing with the surface using several strong strokes of his tail, Zaar directed his followers toward his target with subtle movements of his body. Following Zaar's silent lead, the pack surrounded and then killed the unsuspecting Bull Elephant seal. Injured during an earlier encounter, the bull had had the plain bad luck to meet the Mako near the surface, and only meters away from the shelving safety of the beach. Zaar directed his pack to encircle the injured seal, neatly cutting off any chance for the seal to escape inshore, before leading his henchman in for the kill!

With their bellies filled, at least for the moment, and having eaten their meager share of the kill left to them after the powerful bites and frenzied feeding of their leader, the marauding pack were all too eager to move on, and to taste the blood of their next victim. With his own stomach filled, Zaar continued on his chosen course. Dropping several meters below the surface, they moved as one through the darkened shadows.

Zaar swam slowly. Closing his eyelids he allowed his senses to wander. He enjoyed the raw scents and mixed odors that were being carried by the rush of the flooding tide race.

Rising up slowly in the water, he angled his head up toward the surface to again catch the very faintest of movements. He knew that he swam one tail fluke ahead of his hungry followers. His senses tingled to the discovery that his next victim was swimming quite unaware, and very close by.

Feeling the tip of his dorsal fin break the surface, Zaar closed his mind to all other distractions. With no time to enjoy the feel of the warming sun on his back, he swam to follow the brief sense of movement he had detected in the disturbed seaway ahead of him. Diving beneath the surface, he began to carefully stalk his unseen victim. The surface of the ocean erupted with leaping forms!
The mixed scents of fear and scattered waste marking the terror filled flight of a hundred small lives through the clouded sea. In a foaming volcano of spray and movement, a ragged form flies high into the air, to land with an audible splash on the surface of the sea. The water surrounding the site of this third kill is quickly tinted red with the colour and scent of freshly spilt blood.

Sitting on the exposed rocky outcrops and thin tidal beaches, the small brown forms of many immature Fur seals looked on with large, wet eyes. With his belly full, at least for the moment, Zaar circled through the killing zone, eyeing each of his followers as he swam.

Sensing that they had each fed well, but not too well, he again submerged beneath the sea, as one by one their dorsal fins slowly dipped from view, to once again leave the surface of the water smooth and undisturbed.

Feeling his senses tingle to the faint presence of the life he had detected swimming inside the calm waters of the sheltered bay, Zaar moved slowly through the water, his senses detecting the movement of his unsuspecting prey.

Detecting movement in the water, he enjoyed the shiver as the electric pulses teased the invisible sensors that ran the length of his body. He had felt these tell-tale movements in the water well before his henchmen.

Zaar knew instinctively where to find whatever, or whoever it was causing the disturbance within the calm waters of the sheltered bay that lay just a short swim ahead.

Moving unseen through the sea, Zaar tasted the water for any trace of blood.

But this time it was not the strong scent of blood that had tickled Zaar's senses. Letting himself enjoy the lingering tingle of a very faint taste that was not unknown to him, the sickly sweet scent teased his inquisitive and highly sensitive nose.

Closing the lids over his eyes, he allowed himself to play with the heady scent. The taste fueling his urge to follow the teasing scent trail, and to stalk the life that even now swam unaware of his presence in the sea so close by.

Continuing to swim with caution, Zaar led the trailing pack toward the entrance of the bay. He had chosen to swim closely against the rocky shoreline that plunged deeply, almost vertically downward beneath the waves, the sickly scent continuing to tickle and to tease his senses. Sensing that the others, too, had become aware of whatever it was that had caught his attention, several of the Mako had already moved slightly ahead and under his slow moving body. In a flash of silver, Zaar dropped upon their backs, his huge weight showing them in no uncertain terms that no Mako swam ahead of the all-seeing Zaar.

Slowing himself in the water by reducing the sweep of his tail, Zaar moved in a strangely hypnotic sway. Angling his lateral fins downward, and by using his tail very gently, he swam using the heavy flow of the out-going tides current to keep himself floating almost still in the sea. The other Mako, their previous lesson in manners well-learned, stayed back, swimming in small erratic circles, their unblinking eyes kept fixed to the almost motionless body of their stealthily swimming leader.

 Hidden by a frenzy of early morning feeding, the hazy surface of the bay was marked by a collection of dark humps.
 Floating unmoving in the current, Zaar studied the movements of his prey. The only sound that he could hear was that of the faint noise of the current carrying water and sound across his flanks, and over his sensitive ears. Tensing with excitement as his sensors tingled to his latest discovery, he hung almost motionless in the silty gloom.

Above the distant sounds and clamor that marked the seabirds hungry feeding, he could hear the steady sound of air being forced through a very small space. As each dark hump broke the surface, each expelled air in a tower of light spray. Swimming directly into the current, he counted twelve shadows of varying sizes. Twelve potential targets.

He felt his eye react as the light flashed from each sun tinted body that shone black, each marked with unusual patterns and blobs of stark white. Each slender back was marked by a tall fin or sail. Identifying each sail as they appeared from beneath the sea, showed him that these fish were quite different from each other. The scent here was very strong. Almost overpowering. Zaar followed the movements of the large male. He squinted to the bright glare of the sun as it shone on a tall sail that reached nearly two meters in height, rising up from a rounded back, and high into the early morning sky. With his senses alive to everything around him, Zaar swam to observe more closely.

He watched as the glistening body again broke the surface, his sharpened senses reacting to the noise of venting air.
The hiss of released air sounding short, sharp and powerful. Focusing his eye finally on the source of the scent that continued to excite his nose, Zaar observed the female Orca slowly diving, their unhurried descent leaving trails of silvery tell-tale bubbles dancing above them. He noted their slender sails and their fatted well-rounded tails that marked them as females. He watched the smaller Orca as they fed. He counted three. He only required the killing of one. Already a deadly plan was forming in his hunters mind.

Listening closely to the web of haunting calls, Zaar tasted the lingering scent that had first attracted him to return to this same bay. This was not the scent of blood that had brought him to this place only a few short days before. A visit that he no longer remembered. The sickly sweet scent flooding the waters of the small tidal bay was that of the females' thick, creamy milk, being released into the sea while they fed their young.

Continuing to swim undetected in the rushing tide race, Zaar felt his senses quiver to the high-pitch singing and clicking that was steadily growing louder as he swam ever closer.

Soon he could see his prey. The feeding mothers' swam slowly at a depth of several meters beneath the surface, where they appeared to hang as if they were each suspended in the sea, the suns brightness reflecting in a series of white wobbling lines dancing on their backs. Zaar closed his eyes. He disliked the direct brightness of the sun.

Satisfied that he had found this secret gathering of feeding mothers' and their young, Zaar had to consider that the sounds he was now hearing were a warning that others of their kind may be close by. Allowing himself to drop back with the strength of the current, he swam off to be lost in the swirling currents and foaming wash of the inshore break.

He swam pleased. The young Orca and their weakened nurses made excellent prey to fill their bellies. But he was not so easily fooled. He knew that these whales would be well protected. He swam confident that he could lead an attack against these whales, but first he needed numbers and surprise on his side. And these were things that Zaar could easily arrange. Tearing himself free from his enjoyment of the sickly milk scent, he swam to locate his followers, a lethal and daring plan taking shape within his cold minds-eye.

4.
As the Tor wishes.

The low sea mist clung to the surrounding rocks and cliffs, trapped and unmoving in a windless dawn. The surface of the water within the well-protected bay lay still and hidden beneath a thick blanket of mist. Expecting the return of Rally and Kona from their daily seaward patrol, Torkahn swam concerned for the safety of the younger Kola. Knowing that his eldest son, Rally, tended to be ruled by his heart, and not too often by his head, his fears were soon put to rest as he sensed the far off clicking tones of Rally, forewarning him of the patrols safe return. Some minutes later, through the blue green haze of the outer ocean, Torkahn at last spied the dark shapes of two of his kind.

'I see you, Rally. I see you, Kola! What news from the west?'

Slowing in the water with Kola shadowing his every move as every young bull had been trained to do, Rally swam to make a shallow turn to come about, pushing his body onto the same course and speed of his waiting father.

Checking his speed through the shallow confines of the bay, Rally took care in making sure that he did not allow his head to push in front of that of his silently watching Tor. Kola, as was expected of him, swam back on Rally's left flank.

'I see you, Tor,' toned Rally in greeting. 'We patrolled at your direction, my Tor. First to the north-west where we saw many gluts of the Mackerel. There were cold-bloods taking the slow and the sick as usual, Tor, but they swam quickly on our appearance!' chimed Rally. Kola swam in silence, enjoying his time swimming with Torkahn at the head of the pod.

Feeling pleased with himself, Kola relaxed in the sea as he rose up to take a new breath. Returning beneath the sea, he felt his ear echo to Torkahn's deep tone. The Tor's call took on a steady rumbling as he addressed the two younger bulls.

'Remember my warnings of never underestimating the cold-bloods, Rally. Some of them are pure evil. Some are just plain crazy, but most are just mean,' toned Torkahn, his warning echo sending a quick shiver down Kola's spine.

'Cold blooded means cold hearted, Rally. Mark my tone well.' Rally and Kola exchanged a quick glance as they both obediently toned their understanding of the Tor's solemn warning.

'Now enough of this most serious of lessons, Rally. Tell me, where we can we fill our bellies this day?' called Torkahn, his own belly calling for fish!

'The sea is alive with prey, Tor,' returned Rally.

'We will await Kona's return and his news from the north,' toned Torkahn. 'Then we will swim to the hunt. And perhaps you should lead us today, Kola?' toned Torkahn.

Kola could not believe his ears! He was so excited that he could feel his blood tingling in his veins at the thought of leading a hunt, and of the greasy feast that lay ahead.

Some twenty breaths later Torkahn detected the first distant echoes of Kona's return. Arriving after a long swim, Kona began his report as he swam steadily to take up his position swimming on Torkahn's opposite flank. 'As you please, Tor. Daks relieved me of my patrol, but I regret I have little to report of interest or of benefit to the pod,' toned Kona.

'I may better decide that for myself, Kona, if you would report on your patrol,' toned Torkahn. His deep tone sounding his impatience.

Kona was tired. He also resented being treated as a weed-headed youngster. Drawing in a deep breath he made his report to an impatient Torkahn.

'I travelled close in to the terra, my Tor. Close to the towering outer world where the water boils and thunders. There were seals bathing on the rocks in their countless thousands, Tor, and many of the sky-flyers lying spent on the surface,' toned Kona, his eyes glazing over in memory of the heavy scent of dead seabirds.

After listening to Kona's short report, Torkhan considered all he had heard from his seemingly reluctant scout.

'Thank you, Kona. You may rest now if that is all that you have to report?' toned Torkahn. Kona's eye drifted briefly to rest upon his son, Kola, before he again sent tone to Torkahn. 'On my return journey, Tor, I observed many of the flat-head laying on the sand some hundred breaths distant.'

'Flat-head?' toned Kola, realising he had toned aloud and without the Tor's permission. Kola felt proud to be swimming with the Tor. Keeping pace as he was, swimming in company with the Tor, Rally and his own father, Kona, had given Kola much pride. Kona scowled quietly as his son's youthful enthusiasm, had, for just a brief moment, gotten the better of him. On hearing Kola's interruption, Torkahn rolled his eye back to peer at Kola with a single penetrating eye. Kola felt the hidden strength of Torkahn's stare. Under Torkahn's dark eye, Kola felt himself shrink in the sea as he reduced his speed so that he might just disappear from

Torkahn's view altogether!

'My apologies, Tor,' stammered Kola.

Before he could finish he heard Torkahn's somber tone sounding quietly but firmly.

'Always take care to swim to the order of my van, Kola.'

Dropping back in the sea Rally swam to give Kola a playful nudge and an understanding wink of his friendly eye. Torkahn called for Rally's attention. 'Take Kato and Kola and any of the young ones' who wish to chase the flat-heads. Watch them well, Rally! No heroics or you will answer to their dams,' warned Torkahn.

'I hear and obey, Tor,' returned a very serious toned Rally, hiding his excitement at the prospect of the freedom of ranging away from the pod, and the fun to be had chasing the always elusive flat-heads.

'Be sure that you return before I call for the evening hunt to begin, Rally,' ordered Torkahn.

'As you please, Tor,' toned Rally obediently, the tone of his father's warning echo leaving Rally in no doubt as to the care he should take of the young lives in his charge.

Kola could feel his body shaking with the anticipation and excitement. To Kola, and to all the Orca invited to participate, chasing flat-heads was an unexpected and very rewarding pleasure. Kola followed Torkahn's powerful figure moving with purpose through the sea.

He felt sure that the birth of the Tor's newest son had put Torkahn in a fine mood.

'You are our life, Tor,' boomed Kola, again breaking the strict silence of the van. Torkahn simply shook his head and smiled inwardly, pretending not to have heard the brave young Kola's call. Acting on his father's behalf, Rally swam to again correct, Kola, in a most brotherly way, by simply swimming into him and nudging him away and back towards the idly milling members of the pod. Torkahn knew that the hunt would be good for the young ones. A small celebration for them before the main feed. Swimming close to his attentive mother, an alert Torryn caught sense of Kola's excited tone.

'We swim to hunt the flat-heads,' toned Kola. Seeing Kola rounding up the chattering shapes of Torney and Nayla, Torryn could not contain himself. Having already put on sufficient weight thanks to his mother's rich and nourishing supply of milk, Torryn swam around and around Sorryl in flashes of white, as his high-pitched tone demanded that he too might be allowed to go along on the hunt with his elder brother.

'Oh please, please mother…please, may I go. I promise I shall feed at your side less, and hunt more!' Pined Torryn excitedly. Sorryl's call sounded short and sharp when it came.

'No, Torryn. You are still too young to the great blue to go swimming off in all directions, especially under Rally's tail.' Torryn felt crushed. As if all the air had been taken from his lungs. Nee-Lah, who was swimming close by, gave tone to her own support of Sorryl's decision.

'I am sorry, Torryn, but be sure that your mother knows what is best for you. You must learn to swim to all currents, Torryn. Some are just too strong even for your fine young tail.' Feeling the weight of his disappointment, Torryn swam to the surface to vent and to breathe, his ears ringing to Torney and Nayla's cheerful and teasing tones. It was unfair that he should be left out of all the fun there was to be had in hunting and chasing the flat-headed rays that were such good eating.

Under Rally's watchful eye the younger members of the pod made the swim to the sandy bottomed area of seabed, where an attentive Kona had first reported seeing the giveaway mounds in the sand, which indicated the presence of the always elusive and hiding flat-heads. Having to remain behind and to miss out on his first experience of hunting the flat-heads left Torryn feeling as if he were trapped. How he wished that he, too, could swim free with the others, as they gave chase to the speedy little rays.

Guided by Rally and Kola, Torney and Nayla swam silently together through the shallowing sea, hugging the seabed as they went. Using their noses, Rally and Kola carefully searched the sand in the hunt for their prey. For Rally, finding these tasty treats was the easy part. Teaching Torney and Nayla how to take a ray without getting stung by the dangerous barb in their tails was the hard part! It was something that every young Orca had to learn. Hanging nose down and tail up in the sea, Torney and Nayla watched and waited for the rays that got away, bursting from their sandy cover in a sudden puff of sand and silt, the chase was on!

Feeling as green as the very sea with envy, that the forever pining Torney and Nayla should be the first to experience life away from the always watchful Nee-Lah, Torryn was feeling left out and forgotten. Trapped under the constant care of Nee-Lah and his mother, he was beginning to feel as if he had no control over his own life! He was the son of the Tor, after all. Surely he should be permitted his freedom to hunt with the others?
Having no real understanding of the importance of the rules of the sea, Torryn could feel the strong pull of the depths daring him to set himself free from his ordered life swimming within the guarded safety of the pod.

He had grown tired of swimming in the close company of his mother and Nee-Lah. He never seemed to be able to have just a minute away from the rest of his family. His not being permitted to join the others on the hunt for flat-heads, was for Torryn, the wave that drowned his hopes of his ever having the chance to experience life swimming alone and away from his over protective family.
Sensing the strong lure of the promise of the freedom offered by the open sea, and feeling his tail itching to swim, Torryn made his decision.
 Taking care not be seen, Torryn allowed himself to drop to the seabed where he then swam rapidly toward the sand barred entry to the bay.
Speeding through the clouded water until he thought his lungs would burst, he at last felt that he was free!
 Flying over the sand bar at the entrance to the bay, he swam at speed out into the open sea.
Breaking the surface to take a much needed breathe, he plunged back downward, just as a slow moving school of Snapper swam to cross his course. Charging forward he swam to burst through the teeming throng of fish, scattering the school in a cloud of movement, as he sped on having the time of his young life! With a sudden change in the light, Torryn blinked as the sun shone through a break in the low cloud to reflect on something moving in a bright flash of silver.

Blinking at the warning, he slowed his tail to find himself caught in the gaze of a predator who moved through the water with steady swings of his tail. Torryn held himself rigid! There in the dim light was the unmistakable shape of a shark! Slowing his forward movement in the sea, Torryn froze, certain that he could not avoid the shark's attention. The big Mako had seen him! Torryn had never before set eyes upon such a fish, having only heard his brothers' blood chilling descriptions of these killers. The Mako swam toward him, its eyes black and empty. Jammed in its jaws was the body of a large fur seal. Torryn scented the strong smell of death in the sea. The Mako was trying to make a decision. To let go of the dead seal and give chase to the small Orca, or keep hold of his kill and ignore the foolish young whale. Either way, Torryn recognized the immediate and mortal danger he was in. It was then that he saw a dark shadow pass directly in front of him blocking his view of the Mako.

The inky blackness of the huge shape made the blood in Torryn's tail run cold! Taking his chance, he turned tail to swim faster through the sea than he had while escaping from his mother's overly protective care. Passing back over the bar that marked the entrance to the bay and safety, he finally slowed in the water, refusing to look back.

He knew that he had escaped death by a very narrow margin. Managing to calm his racing heart, he swam to return to his place swimming at his mother's side. Relaxing into the rhythm of the pod, Torryn turned his mind to consider that whatever it was that had passed before him had saved his life. Oddly, he found that he had felt no real fear, or even a sense of threat when confronted by the Mako. He swam with a strong feeling that he should have recognized the presence of whatever, or whoever it was, that had swum between him and the oncoming shark. It had saved him. He recognized that either the shark, or the dark shadow that had moved in front of him in warning, could quite easily have ended his short life there and then. With his first attempt to leave the pod ending in near fatal and dangerous failure, Torryn swam certain that he would not try to leave the security of the pod alone again. The usually always attentive Nee-Lah had not noticed Torryn's absence from his mother's side. Seeking Torryn's familiar form in the shallow water of the bay, Nee-Lah had a sense that something was amiss with her newest responsibility, as Torryn had suddenly become quiet, and was swimming close to Sorryl's side. She would have to keep a watchful eye on her young charge in the future, she thought to herself. Like his father, the great Torkahn, Torryn-Gah had a mind of his own. Thanking all the stars above that he had not been missed, Torryn knew that he would have to be much more careful next time, if there was ever to be a next time. He knew now that his own life depended on it.

5.
Call of the blue.

After six short weeks spent swimming in the safety of the shallow waters of Shelter Bay, Torkahn could see that Sorryl was losing body weight, and that Torryn, judging by his rapid increase in size, was now more than ready to swim with, and to keep up with the main body of the pod. Torryn too was growing restless.
 The small bay that was his home was becoming smaller by the day. Nee-Lah marveled that Torryn's birth size had almost doubled due to the benefit of the nourishment provided by his mother's nourishing milk. Torkahn watched Torryn from a distance. He could feel the call of the deep. He sensed that it would soon be time for him to move the pod on - on to the next leg of their yearly journey.
 The previous evening Torryn had watched the dark sky grow darker. The masses of swirling black cloud, heavy with the rain that fell like sheets of silver pilchards from the sky, met the swell of the sea, driven by a whipping wind, in an awesome blast of power. Torryn swam

thankful to be swimming in the protection of his mother and Nee-Lah's solid bodies, as the wind howled over their backs to bend their sails each time they surfaced to snatch another hurried breath. Enjoying the feeling of the pattering rain upon his back, Torkahn moved with little effort through the deepening swells, calling to the pod as he made preparations to lead them out to sea for the morning's feeding.

Earlier in the pre-dawn dusk, Torkahn had sent for Rally and Kato, directing them to swim out ahead of the pod to scout for suitable feeding schools. Noticing Kola swimming silently and alone, Torkahn watched as Kola swam trailing Kato and Rally on their way to their duty. He sensed Kola's disappointment at his not having been chosen to accompany Kato and Rally on that mornings scout. Kola glided silently past Torkahn's eye without sounding his usual greeting. Seeing how low Kola carried his head, Torkahn sent quiet tone to the younger whale.

'You led us well to the hunt, Kola. I have not forgotten you. Your time will come soon enough. You must learn to be patient, young one.' On hearing Torkahn address him, Kola straightened visibly in the sea. He would wait. His time would come.

Each morning Torkahn would begin his day by seeking out Sorryl, and the now not so little

Torryn. This morning was no different. He swam through the early morning gloom, his eyes fixed on Sorryl, as he moved to gently rub his head along her smooth flanks, his own personal gesture of love and recognition to his mate.

'I see you, Sorryl, and I see you, too, young, Torryn-Gah,' toned Torkahn. Torryn had come to look forward to these rare visits by his tall-sailed father.

'I hear you, Tor,' Torryn piped excitedly, his immature tone, and the faltering way he delivered his piercing greeting to his father, showing Torkahn that his son was indeed a quick learner. This was important. As it meant that Torryn had a chance at survival in the open sea.

Over the first several weeks of Torryn's life, Torkahn had watched closely as Torryn was taught the language of the Tor-Gah under Nee-Lah's patient instruction. Feeling his ear ring to Torryn's early morning call, Torkahn could hear in the urgency and high pitch of his son's call, that Torryn had learned very quickly how to make himself heard!

'Oh, Tor, please may I join the morning hunt?' Whined Torryn. 'I have grown strong, father, and I have already doubled my weight!'

Arching his back in the sea as if to give extra height to his still stubby sail, Torryn waited for his father to reply. Torkahn winked his smiling eye. He was already well acquainted with his newest son's progress. At his order, Nee-Lah swam to join him each evening to report directly to him on the progress being made in both the tuition and physical well-being of each young member of the pod.

'I hear you, Torryn-Gah, mighty hunter,' toned Torkahn, his call sounding to Torryn in playful jest.

'Please, Tor, do not mock him. He has his father's impatience to be on the swim,' piped Sorryl.

'Soon, soon young one,' toned Torkahn in reply to his newest son's eager call.

'Today I shall lead the feeding and leave you here to guard your mother and the others while I am away, Torryn. On tomorrow's dawn we shall leave this place and return to the blue.' Torkahn's deep tone hung in the water to fill Torryn's head with information that he could not quite process.

'To the blue?' Torryn toned softly, realising that with the coming of tomorrow's dawn would come his greatest test, as he would be swimming with the pod in the open sea as it continued its long journey northward, toward the warmer waters of the Tor's crowded and always inviting spring feeding grounds.

Overcome at hearing such incredible news, Torryn sped around the pod, swimming from whale to whale, all the time chattering excitedly! 'Tomorrow I swim the blue!' he piped, to any whale who would listen. Swimming by Kona and Kola, Torryn sensed Kona's dark eye following him through the sea. Not wishing to show deliberate disrespect to his elder, Torryn toned his greeting to Kona as he past.

'I see you, Kona,' Torryn called. Kona eyed Torryn before making his reply to Torryn's enthusiastic greeting.

'I hear you, Torryn-Gah,' returned Kona, his own tone sounding deep and menacing. Torryn found that he had to strain his senses to hear what the elder Orca had toned as he swam by.

'Do not swim far from your mother, young Tor. For you will surely perish out there in the blue.' Torryn did not know what to make of this. He was not even sure that he had heard anything at all. But that deep tone had just managed to reach his ear. Whether he was meant to hear it or not, he thought that Kona was, as was the way with most of the elder bulls, perhaps just teasing him. Swimming to put this strange event out of his mind, Torryn felt a new sensation deep within himself. It was a dark feeling that seemed alive in the pit of his belly. And it was not, Torryn thought to himself, because he was feeling hungry.

Waiting until an excited Torryn had returned to his mother, and out of tones range, Kona toned silently to Kola.

'That young pup needs knocking back before he grows too large for his sail!' Kola was concerned as he listened with unease to his father's whispered tones. Although his father was near thirty cycles in age, Kola swam aware that no Tor-Gah should tone ill of the Tor's youngest son. Kola was about to tone his thoughts to his silently brooding father, until he saw the look in his father's dark eye. It scared Kola to think that such bad feeling should be alive within the pod. And that his own father should hold such feelings.

Having given the order for the pod to move into formation, Torkahn sent tone for Kola. Answering Torkahn's call, Kola obediently left Kona's side, giving a small dip of his head as a gesture of respect to his father as he swam away. Feeling a weight lift from his tail, Kola swam eager to taste fresh water, and to join Torkahn at the head of the pod.

'I answer your call, Tor,' toned Kola. His excitement at swimming beside his tall sailed leader while he awaited Torkahn's instruction gave him a feeling of heavy responsibility. If he ever wished to swim at the head of the pod as those older and more experienced than he did, he must first prove his ability and worth to Torkahn.

Torkahn's cool stare upon him reminded Kola that the Tor was indeed master of all he surveyed. Kola swam ready.

'You will not be joining this morning's hunt, Kola. Your duty will be to me directly. You are to remain here to guard the dams and the young ones,' toned Torkahn.

'I need a trusted bull to look after the very Life-blood of the pod, Kola. See that you are not seen by my son, but patrol the mouth of the bay and stay in easy breath of the dam.'

Torkahn waited for Kola's response. He wanted to be sure that Kola had understood the importance of his orders.

'As the Tor pleases,' answered Kola, his serious tone sounding the importance of his duty to Torkahn's ear. Although he had been anxious to swim in the lead position on that morning's hunt, and although he did feel somewhat disappointed at his again having missed his opportunity to join in, Kola swam proud in the knowledge that the Tor was giving him an opportunity to prove his loyalty to the pod, and most importantly of all, loyalty to the Tor himself. Returning to Kona to report on this great honour that the Tor had bestowed upon him, Kola found his father looking cool and ill at ease as he listened to his son's news.

Staring into the depths Kona hissed his harsh reply.

'Lower your tail, Kola. Do not celebrate the fact that the great Tor has made you a baby sitter!' Kona swam in close to Kola, his ominous tone sounding very quietly. 'You were born to better things, my son. You should be on the point, swimming with Rally and Daks, not cooling your tail back here with the females and the Torryn brat!'

Knowing that it was not his place to answer his father back, Kola sent out a nervous tone. 'But father,' his young tone so quiet that even Kona had trouble hearing his son's urgent call. 'I do not have enough cycles behind me to demand such a place.' Kona shifted in the sea, turning his eye toward his son. At that very moment Torkahn's booming signal interrupted Kola's stilted call. Closing his eyes Kona listened.

'I see you, Kona. Perhaps you do not wish to feed this morning, but I have a hungry pod to feed.' Shifting himself in the sea, Kona turned to see Torkahn's shaded silhouette appear briefly through the gloom, his huge shadow moving quickly and impatiently as he swam to muster the hunt. 'I hear you, Tor and I obey,' returned Kona. As Torkahn disappeared from sight, Kona rose in the sea. 'Bah,' he hissed, his obvious displeasure muffled as he briefly raised his head above water, shot out a brief breath of stale air with a resounding hiss, before again submerging, and allowing his all-seeing eye to lock on to that of his son.

'Mark my tone, Kola. You have more brains and knowledge than Rally has in his small eye.' With several strong pushes of his tail, Kona swam from Kola's sight, out into the blue, where he swam to take up his usual station on the left rear side of the Tor's eager hunting pack.

Observing Kona appearing through the murk in answer to his call, Torkahn thought about the often silent Kona. Kona was only several years younger than himself. His sail was not quite as tall as that of his own, but through his actions and service, Kona had proven that he was loyal to the pod. Kona was a strong swimmer and an excellent hunter. Searching his memory, Torkahn turned his thoughts back to the day Kona had first joined the Tor-Gah.
Born into the Gah-Toh pod, Kona was descended from another family of ocean wanderers led by another tall sailed Tor, and an ally to Torkahn, named Gah-Lah.
'I hear you, Tor and I obey,' returned Kona. As Torkahn disappeared from sight, Kona rose in the sea.
'Bah,' he hissed, his obvious displeasure muffled as he briefly raised his head above water, shot out a brief breath of stale air with a resounding hiss, before again submerging, and allowing his all-seeing eye to lock on to that of his son.

But this was none of Torkahn's business, as the personal affairs of his bulls were theirs and theirs alone, unless that behaviour began to have a direct impact on the everyday lives of the members of the pod.

Torkahn's loyalty to those who swam with him was absolute. He had heard Sorryl give tone to stories echoed by others of the pod concerning the often quiet and brooding Kona. He would not give his ear to storytelling, or to the idle currents of rumor within the pod. He knew that his cousin Lae-nah, Kola's mother, had sought the company of another smaller pod, and that the female had left the Gah-Toh voluntarily and alone, some weeks before Kona and Kola's return to them. With Torkahn's blessing, Kona swam to take up his previous position within the pod. Welcoming Kona and Kola as valued members of the Tor-Gah, Torkahn saw the advantages of acquiring two bulls, who each, in their own way, added much in the way of help, especially when it came to the daily tasks of feeding, guiding, and most importantly of all, of defending the pod.

Aware that he had been letting his thoughts drift, Torkahn turned his attention to leading the pod out from the shelter of the isolated and rain swept bay. Unused as he was to feeling unsure of himself, he swam with a feeling of apprehension at his having to leave the females and the young, alone and at the mercy of the sea.

Forcing these thoughts from his mind, Torkahn swam confident that the females of the pod were each more than capable when it came to defending themselves and their young. Yet the nagging doubt that lingered in his mind continued to distract his thoughts.

With his nose pushing slowly ahead in front of his hunting pack, he found a brief moment to consider his own mate. A shimmering image of Sorryl danced teasingly before his eyes. Torkahn worried for his graceful Sorryl. Her slender appearance a sign that she had yet to return to the hunt to feed following Torryn's birth. At their last meeting, Torkahn had noticed how Sorryl's previously rounded and fattened bulk was at last beginning to show the first signs of weakness and hunger. Since Torryn's birth, Sorryl had been living off her own body fat so that she was able to stay with, and suckle Torryn, until they were both ready to return to the freedom and tasty rewards of the blue.

Slowing in the water, Torkahn's last sight was of Kola, his form a blur of movement in the sea. Watching Kola drop from the rear of the pod, Torkahn allowed his eye to follow Kola as he swam to take up his allotted patrol position, swimming as he had been ordered, to patrol the waters across the broad and rain swept mouth of the sheltered bay.

Giving his last thoughts to his lovely Sorryl, the two young dams, Sey-la and Soh-nee, and their calves, Torkahn pictured Torryn's image, swimming with his mother, alone now in calm and protected waters. Torkahn swam secure in the knowledge that he had left Kola close by. As an added precaution, Nee-Lah had chosen to give up her place in that morning's hunt, in order for her to remain behind in support of Sorryl and Torryn. Still feeling uneasy, Torkahn swam with some small confidence that his family swam well protected from any lurking danger in his absence.

6.
Where danger lurks!

An uncomfortable feeling deep inside him warned Torkahn that perhaps he had forgotten, or not foreseen something. It was a feeling that he always swam weary of, because he knew that he should never risk second guessing his own decisions. He had entrusted Kola with a grave responsibility. He must stand by his choice. Of this there could be no question. He trusted Kola, and he had taken every precaution.

Swimming on his patrol across the mouth of Shelter Bay, Kola moved through the sea taking great care not to be seen by those he was charged to protect as Torkahn had ordered. Kola felt his senses tingle and strain under the full weight of his responsibility. Swimming wide-eyed and awake to all of the hidden dangers that lurked in the sea all around him, he swam his course, alert and ready to face any threat.

The shelving mouth of Shelter Bay was broad and shallow. The distance between the two wind-swept and isolated headlands was a short swim of two breaths, a distance Kola knew could be covered in a few minutes swimming.

Moving through the sea using steady strokes of his tail, Kola remembered how he and Rally had surprised the Mako in these same waters only a few days before. Taking a deep breath and sending power to his tail, he swam to cover his patrol line as he had been ordered to do, taking the greatest care to not make any unnecessary sound that may give away his presence in the sea. He knew that to a cold-blood, movement was an indication of life, and to a shark, any life meant prey.

Swimming unseen not far away, were the first signs of danger. A group of cold-bloods led by a large male with a scarred back, cruised submerged, hidden from sight beneath the ruffled surface of the sea. Swimming with stealth across the broad mouth of the bay, the wily Mako knew that their shaded outlines would be hidden from view, shielded by the murky turbulence caused by the constantly rolling breakers and the swiftly running tide.

Having reformed the remains of his rag-tag band of followers far out to sea, Zaar also swam with a similar feeling of unease. Swimming a broad circular course, their travel had returned them to the site where Zaar's keen senses had first detected signs of life in the shelving safety of the small bay.

Swimming across the mouth of the bay he still could not shake the nagging feeling of unease. His sensors tingling to an unmistakable warning. Though he could not identify the looming sense of threat, his small, efficient brain told him that it was perhaps a trick of the crashing waves breaking against the cliffs and stony beaches. With his companions circling in impatient arcs around him, Zaar's senses caught and locked onto Kola's figure, swimming silently submerged across the mouth of the bay. Using his quick thinking hunter's brain, Zaar had already guessed correctly that the patrolling Orca would have to slow in the churning waters to swim about, before he could begin to swim the next northward leg of his long duty. It was at this precise moment that Zaar made the instant decision to pass through the shallow passage across the bar which led into the somewhat deeper and more sheltered basin of the bay. Hugging the opposite shoreline Zaar and his pack moved ever closer and undetected to their unsuspecting prey.

Swimming blissfully unaware of the drama unfolding only a few short breaths away, Torryn was having the time of his small life! He was busy enjoying playing tag with the long-suffering flat-heads, and if any whale could find and reveal the well-hidden flat-fish, it was Torryn.

Hunting the sandy bottom in company with always excitable Torney and Nayla, Torryn was enjoying flushing the remaining rays from their sandy hiding places, and from under the noses of his hungry competition. Torney and Nayla were like sisters to him. Though older than he was by a full season, they each enjoyed chasing him and making him the center of one of their often silly games. Torryn could see them poking half-heartedly in the sand as if they were not really interested. He could tell that they were watching him out of the corner of their eye.

Torney and Nayla bumped along the bottom of the bay, nose down, as they slowly moved closer to Torryn. As they drew ever nearer, Torryn felt his ear echo to Nayla's painfully high pitched call. 'His sail is still very stubby, sister,' she called to Torney. 'Not at all the sail of a Tor!' teased Torney in reply. 'And surely he is not growing any longer, but only more round with the passing of each fresh tide!' piped Nayla.

Doing his best to ignore them, Torryn tried to close his ears to Torney's piercing tone. It was true that he did spend a lot of time feeding from his mother, and the result was beginning to show in the form of his rapid growth. He had already grown to six times his birth size. He was sure that his sail had grown taller, and that his tail was filling out. And more importantly, he was eating more fish. Growing bored with Torryn pretending that they were invisible, Torney and Nayla swam to return to their mothers' sides, the water filling with the whining twang of calves who were hungry.

Comparing his growth to theirs, Torryn could see that the twins, too, had each grown to the right size and weight for their mothers' to finally begin weaning the pair from their dependence on their rich supply of milk. The two young females were growing quickly, and were of an age where they must begin to learn the art of survival if they were ever going to be capable of taking care of themselves and swimming as independent members of the pod.

Knowing that this was the time, both Sey-la and Soh-nee had arranged for Nee-Lah to begin teaching the twins the art of the chase, while assisting them with the mastering of their most unique of natural abilities, the Orca science of echo-location.

Upon their hearing that theywould both have to attend Nee-Lah's lessons each morning, Torney and Nayla whined in protest, until Nee-Lah herself put an end to their tuneless complaining. For Sey-la and Soh-nee, the twin's lessons could not come quickly enough.

Growing bored, Torryn returned to swim quietly at Sorryl's side.

'I see you small one,' toned Sorryl in greeting. 'Tomorrow, Torney and Nayla begin their lessons with Nee-Lah. You will be lonely without their company, I know, Torryn. So, I have arranged for you to attend Nee-Lah's instruction, together with the Torney and Nayla. This will give you a good head start in life. Your father has agreed that you should take part,' Sorryl told him.

Torryn swam stunned! He had been looking forward to swimming in peace and having the entire bottom of the bay to himself, free from Torney and Nayla's teasing and noisy games for a few short hours' every day.

Sensing that Torryn was thinking of a way to avoid joining Torney and Nayla the following morning, Sorryl gave tone to her final call.

'Your father and I both feel that it is important that you should attend Nee-Lah's lessons, Torryn. Your father will soon be ready to lead us away from here to continue on our journey. It is best that you do all that you can to prepare for what will be a very long swim in open sea.'

Torryn felt trapped! His first sign of freedom had been snatched away as quickly as it had arrived. All he could do now was obey his parent's wishes.

'I hear you, mother,' he toned in reluctant obedience.

'Nee-Lah will be expecting you in the morning one hour after sun up,' returned Sorryl.

'I know that you will do your best, Torryn. And that you will make your father proud.'

The following morning, and with a heavy tail, Torryn swam to join Torney and Nayla as they floated patiently awaiting Nee-Lah's instruction to begin. Appearing from out of the blue, Nee-Lah swam to a stop, her nose coming very close to her three new students. Torney was playfully nudging Torryn as Nee-Lah's tone filled their ears.

'Now you must listen and learn. It is my task to awaken within each of you the talents that you will need to survive in our sea. You are whales' of the Tor-Gah, and as such you must learn to hunt, swim and survive in the open sea.

The Tor has entrusted your lives and education to me, so you will each watch, listen and learn. You will do as I tell you and do your best for me, and for your Tor. Do you understand?' Torney, Nayla and Torryn each hung in the sea as they listened to Nee-Lah's short speech. Their lives were about to change, that much they knew. None of them wished to be the whale that let down the Tor. Bowing their heads as one, they each promised Nee-Lah that they would do their best.

Beginning her first lesson by creating a ball of high-pitched sound deep within her enlarged nasal cavity, Nee-Lah then fired this ball of directed sound far out ahead of her into the sea. Torney, Nayla and Torryn each watched her in quiet fascination. Recognising that she at last had their attention, Nee-lah looked to Torryn.

'It is your turn to try now, Torryn,' she toned. Closing his eyes, Torryn tried very hard to form his own ball of sound. His first attempts resulting in little burps of sound that made Torney and Nayla giggle. Soon all three of them were practicing forming and sending their own unique signals. Torryn became very competitive. Trying to out-do Torney and Nayla in both sound and distance.

Learning that there were many advantages to having mastered this art, Torryn quickly discovered the fun to be had by firing off short bursts of sound at the flat and undisturbed bottom of Shelter Bay. He enjoyed the thrill of watching the results of his small pings, as the invisible balls of sound touched the sandy bottom of the bay, causing tiny puffs of sand and silt, and revealing as if by magic, the previously hidden forms of those flat-heads brave enough to risk living and hiding beneath the sand in the shallow waters of Shelter Bay.

Swimming relaxed through the sea, Sorryl, Soh-nee and Sey-la rolled their bodies in the water to allow the warming rays of the sun to tickle their shining flanks. With the wind dropping and the morning's rain squalls having passed over, Sorryl continued to float, enjoying the quiet time, while Torney, Nayla and Torryn cruised around beneath her, under the ever watchful gaze of the always attentive Nee-Lah.
The young trio practiced their hunting in the soft sand, while trying to outdo each other in just how long they could each hold their breath, before they were forced to return to the surface to breathe. The calm waters of the bay echoed to Sorryl's tunefully echoed songs. Torryn enjoyed hearing his mother's reassuring tones, her musical call sounding beneath the tranquil water of the peaceful bay

Sorryl had taught him that these songs and stories were the living history of the Tor-Gah, as they had been taught to her by Nee-Lah. Each song told the story of a memory about the lives of the now departed, but never to be forgotten members of their ancient undersea family. Songs, that with the passing of time and tide, each member of the pod would come to know, remember, and then pass on to others of their kind, over the seasons and tides to come. This was their way.

Moving swiftly and still unseen through the seaway as they stayed close to the shore, Zaar led his followers into the security and calmer water of the bay, his sharpened senses tensing as Sorryl's highly pitched calls increased in strength in his ears. Moving only meters beneath the surface of the water, Zaar angled his body to briefly check that his followers were still swimming in their positions. Satisfied, he swam ready to launch his surprise attack.

Having successfully managed to avoid detection by Kola who swam patrolling the mouth of the bay, Zaar could not believe his own good luck! All that remained for him to do now, was to lead his jumpy band in for the kill!

7.
The Attack!

Leading the hunt some miles distant, Torkahn felt a sudden sense of foreboding creeping up his spine. Feeling a sudden shiver which began at the base of his sail and spread slowly down his arching flanks, Torkahn took this sense for what it was. An unmistakable warning. Acting on this warning, he sent strong tone for Kona. In less than a breath Kona appeared to swim at Torkahn's side, his snout pushing the sea upward in a wash of small wavelets as he toned his respectful greetings.

'You will leave the pod, Kona, and return with all speed to the females and the young,' instructed Torkahn. This was not at all what Kona had wanted to hear. 'Trouble, Tor?' toned Kona. 'Surely, my son, Kola is on hand to....' Torkahn's urgent tone silenced Kona's plea before its echo had died in their wake. With no time to discuss his concerns, the set of Torkahn's call left Kona in no doubt that he should act on the Tor's command immediately.

'If you leave now you can be with them in good time,' urged Torkahn. Meeting Torkahn's eye, Kona could sense that it was useless to attempt to sway the Tor from his quick decision. With a flick of his tail Kona turned in the sea to set course for the near distant waters of Shelter Bay.

Kona had not appreciated the Tor's harsh tone. Neither did he appreciate being ordered to return to the females and the young with such undue haste. He was a proud whale. The Tor treating him as a scatter headed youth did not please him. The thought of having to return to the Tor's female and the Torryn brat made his pounding heart beat even faster. He was no babysitter. He was a hunting bull of the Tor-Gah! He was an ocean hunter feared by many and respected by all. As he sailed through a lightening sea, the first dark currents of a daring plan began to form in Kona's mind. Slowing in the sea he swam at a more relaxed pace. He would not tire himself to no good purpose. The Tor's mate and brat could wait.

Sensing that Kola swam somewhere nearby, his presence hidden in the green murk of the sea, Zaar moved through the clouds of disturbed plant life, driftwood, and the very small creatures that were the very life of the sea. Knowing that these whales' hunted in complete silence, Zaar slowed in the water, listening.

Leading his small band of silent followers through the murky waters of the entry to the bay, Zaar sensed that Kola had failed to detect their movement through the racing tide. Sweeping his head from side to side, Zaar bought his nose about to quickly change his heading. Moving with a deliberate purpose, he swam closer toward the rocky shore and to the shelter offered by the screening sound and constant motion of the breaking sea against the rocks. Angling his head upward he shielded his eyes, adjusting his sight quickly to the rapid change in light.

Zaar led the shadowy group as they closed on the dimly lit surface, the rough motion of the sea echoing the temper of the weather above them as a fresh rain squall pelted the waters of the bay. The grey and overcast sky providing Zaar with just the visibility he required.

Surfacing close to his mother, Torryn felt the sudden sting of the strong southerly wind on his back as it lashed this exposed side of the bay. Listening to the sound of the scattered rain returning to pelt the sea in a constant tattoo, he dipped beneath the waves where he could only faintly hear the crackling as the slanting raindrops were hungrily swallowed by a wind-swept sea.

Feeling his senses quiver to the scents in the surrounding waters tainted with the scent of the rich milk of the female Orca, Zaar tasted and tested this collection of scents in his brain, before returning his attention to the Orca guarding the mouth of the bay. He knew that it would take no little time for the still unsuspecting Kola to return to the defence of the nursing females, but that small window of opportunity was all that Zaar required.

His spine quivered as he sensed that four females and three calves of the Tor-Gah swam little more than a dash away. Zaar intended to carry out his attack with lightning speed. He would first startle the females with several very close passes to be made by the three larger Mako in his pack. With jerking movements of his muscular body Zaar signed his orders to the remaining three of his followers. They would swim in low and under the dams to attack at the calves from beneath, in the keen hope of drawing first blood. Hearing, but not understanding the rather annoying singing and clicking that bounced off every rock in the bay, Zaar felt his ears vibrate to the friendly and playful calls of his prey. He was doubly pleased that his targets were providing him with the perfect means for him to be able to track in on their exact locations.

Swimming unaware that he was in immediate danger, Torryn continued to swim nose down near the sandy bottom, swimming directly under the long shadows being cast by his mother and Nee-Lah. With his snout buried in the seabed, his stubby tail waving slowly back and forth, he moved along the sandy bottom examining each of his latest finds. Hidden by small clouds of sand, he searched gamely for his next rewarding snack of shellfish, or the promise of yet another game of dash with the flat-heads.

It was at this exact moment Zaar chose to launch his sudden and ferocious assault! The deadly change in sound came as a brutal shock to Torryn! The sea was suddenly alive with the squeals and screams of the shocked females and their young, as the deadly steel grey shapes of the cold-bloods rushed in at incredible speed over the top of Torryn's head. The always alert Nee-Lah was the first to detect the sudden and hidden danger! Before she could echo a tone of warning, she moved her body to cover Torney and Nayla from the impact of Zaar's first attack. Leading three Mako in a rapid frontal attack in an attempt to pass between Sorryl and Sey-la, Zaar threw his strong body against the silky smooth and exposed flank of a shocked Sorryl. Wincing at the graze of Zaar's rough skin on her side, Sorryl felt the first shiver of real fear. Not a fear for herself, but a fear born of motherhood, and a strong maternal desire to protect her young. As the Mako made their first rapid pass, Sorryl's urgent tone called for the two young ones to stay within the solid protection of Sey-la and herself, calling for Nee-Lah and Soh-nee to dive, and to use their bodies to shield a petrified Torney and Nayla. Sorryl, her eyes darting everywhere and with her blood rushing at a much increased rate, swam angrier now than scared! She had no idea where Torryn was, but she knew that he was not here, with her, where he should be!

Turning her thoughts to Torkahn, who was then leading the pod to the hunt far away to the north, Sorryl saw his image clearly in her minds-eye. Nee-Lah struck out at one of the Mako, her mouth hanging open to reveal her bared teeth. Just like Sorryl, the loyal and loving Nee-Lah would fight to the death to defend her family.
'Oh Torkahn, great Tor, we need you now,' pined Sorryl, her feminine tone sounding in an urgent shriek, as she positioned her body to shield the exposed and vulnerable Torney and Nayla from the sickening force of Zaar's next attack. Hearing his mother's urgent call, Torryn reacted to the bright silver flashes of the cold-bloods shattering the bays peaceful calm. From his position swimming close to the seabed, he caught a brief glimpse of the three smaller Mako

swimming in fast and unseen, as they swam close to the seabed to hide their sneaking approach. Trying to keep his attackers in view, Torryn watched as they each swam wide- eyed and unblinking, ready to launch their own surprise attack from below, in their hope of breaking through the protective defence of the combined bulk of his mother and her companions.

Not really knowing what to do, or how to act, Torryn swam sure of only one thing. That his father had told him that he was responsible for the safety of his mother and the others while he was away leading the pod. Thinking of the great trust that his father had placed in him, Torryn knew that there was only one thing that he could do, and that was to defend his mother and his family with all of his strength and ability. He knew by instinct that his family were swimming blind to this second attack. His instinct for own survival telling him that this new attack would be enough to distract the females from holding their positions, while sheltering the young calves against the sharp teeth of the four larger cold-bloods.

In his mind, Torryn saw how this attack could separate the group, leaving spaces large enough for the sharp-toothed Mako to strike through. Feeling a shiver run the length of his body, he sent urgent strength to his tail as he raced along with a renewed courage, moving rapidly and still unseen by the three quickly approaching sharks. With the sound of his own beating heart pounding in his ears, he swam to meet his targets head-on!

Hearing the panicked calls of the females and the young, Kola sent every ounce of his strength to his tail. In an instant he was speeding through the cloudy water, afraid that he may arrive too late to prevent the unthinkable! The Tor had charged him with the care and protection of his young. To fail the Tor and his father now would mean a disgrace that he could not bear to think about!

Swimming nose down, Torryn bravely faced his attackers. He could feel the sea rushing over his body, his eyes taking constant snap shots of the incoming Mako. He watched the sudden upward movement made by the attacking sharks as they each changed their heading, swimming almost in unison with their noses up, in their attempt to break through the defences of the small pod. As he watched, Torryn realized that each incoming Mako would have to briefly expose their pale and unprotected bellies as they swam upward to attack from directly beneath his mother and the others.

With his blood rushing and knowing that the last of his precious air was nearly spent, Torryn launched himself forward with strong thrusts of his tail.

As the three cold-bloods came on, their blood-lust blinding them to everything, except their combined risk of failure in the eyes of the ever threatening Zaar. Seeing Nee-Lah using her own body to shield Torney and Nayla from the force of the attack, Torryn again caught sight of the fast moving cold-bloods as they closed in for the kill. Feeling his entire body electrified with a sudden feeling of great strength, he allowed his jaw to hang open, revealing the small mounds of his still undeveloped teeth. Swimming still unseen, he aimed his snout toward the first two Mako. Trying not to tense himself for the staggering impact, he felt his snout punch hard into the exposed belly of the leading shark! Shuddering to the blow, he swam under and away from the stunned Mako. Twisting in the sea as he sent all strength to his tail, he slammed head first into the solid flank of the second oncoming shark. The impact on his body of slamming head first into the second shark left Torryn swimming dazed and momentarily unaware of his surroundings. Caught unawares, he arched in the water as he felt a searing pain just behind his sail as the third shark sank its teeth into his unprotected back.

Just as Sorryl thought that all was lost, an explosion of noise, wake and bubbles left her senses clouded by a blur of movement! Knowing Torkahn would not have left them completely alone without the added benefit of a watchful eye, Sorryl watched a dark shape shoot by her at speed. She could not identify the whale that had moved through the sea only meters from where she now swam. Her only worry was for he son, Torryn. It was then that she saw below her the familiar shape of her son. As she looked on helplessly, her big heart pounding, she watched in shocked horror Torryn's head-on collision with the charging form of a cold-blood! Terror stricken, she watched the last Mako sink its teeth into the exposed back of her only offspring. Distracting her for a second, Sorryl heard Kola's call as she felt the motion of his powerful tail as he sped by her and in to the attack!

Catching the Mako with a heavy blow to the gills, Kola's stunning hit killed the attacker instantly. Its body stunned rigid, the dead shark fell slowly to the waiting sand below. With no time to check on Torryn, Kola increased his speed, swimming upward towards the surface in search of the other fish who had dared to challenge the might of the Tor-Gah. All he found were the stilled forms of two of the larger cold-bloods. Kola watched in a mild daze as their bodies sank slowly, to come to rest, unmoving, on the sandy bottom of the bay.

Of the other attackers, there was no sign. For a brief instant, Kola had caught a fleeting glimpse of a large Mako, the sun flashing from his silvery hide as it sped from view to be lost in the murk of the sea. Kola recognized the Mako by just that quick glimpse. He knew that it was the same fish who had come off second best in its collision with Rally some days earlier. In the same thought, he knew deep within himself, that this would not be last time that the bullying Mako swam across their course.

With the danger over, Kola felt his fighting senses begin to calm as he swam to join the small, and by now greatly relieved nursery pod. Torney and Nayla were all a chatter at having just missed a grizzly death by seconds. Sey-la and Soh-nee, too, were equally impressed and relieved at their very narrowest of escapes. Sorryl swam gently, guiding Torryn as she examined the fresh wound on his injured back.
'I see you, Kola,' piped a very relieved Sorryl. 'I thank you for your most timely of arrivals. Surely we would all have perished had it not been for your brave action this day!'
The sea echoed with the females songs of praise until Kola could suffer it no longer.
'I hear you, Sorryl, dam of Torkahn-Gah,' Kola returned in a dutiful tone.

'Do not thank me so quickly, my lady, for it was your own son, Torryn, who has slain several of these beasts.' Kola swam down to examine the corpses of the dead Mako lying dead on the sandy bottom, their eyes fixed, their gaping jaws stilled forever.

It was then that Kola heard his father's deep tone. Kona's easily recognizable shape appeared out of the gloom, his strong body sliding effortlessly through the sea as he circled the scene, his surprised eye counting the now stilled bodies of the dead Mako, whose shattered corpses moved eerily to the pull of the bottom currents.

'I see you, father,' toned Kola, as he swam to join his father. Kona's eyes were everywhere.

'It seems that the Tor was right to have me return to look after you,' toned Kona.

'Four cold-bloods are no more, father,' called Kola.

'And not a mark upon you?' returned Kona in surprise.

'I did not act alone, father.' Kona eyed the females closely.

'You are to be congratulated. I would expect no more from the Tor's lady,' toned Kona.

'No, father. It was Torryn who claimed two of these devils!' called Kola.

'Torryn?' hissed Kona in disbelief.

'Yes, Kona,' piped Sorryl, feeling her tone shaking from the nervous excitement and stress of the sudden and unexpected attack. 'My small, Torryn. He has received a wound, Kona. The Tor will wish to know why his youngest son has been exposed to such danger.' Kona peered at Torryn and saw the small wound and the torn skin behind Torryn's sail.

'It is but a scratch, but still a fine mark on one so young,' toned Kona.

Sorryl could not believe that Kona appeared to be so unconcerned at seeing Torryn's injury, or how close the young had come to so grisly a death.

Choosing to ignore Sorryl's tone, Kona turned his disapproving eye on Kola.

'You did not detect the presence of these cold-bloods, Kola?' he toned accusingly. Kola backed in the sea, hanging his head at the harshness of his father's call.

'I am sorry, father, but I did not,' returned Kola, his call sounding hushed as he tried hard not to meet his father's eye. Sensing that Kona was being far too harsh on Kola, Sey-la and Soh-nee each rose to his defence.

'And where were you, Kona, when we had urgent need of you?' sang Sey-la.

'It seems you leave the dangerous duty to the young!' toned Soh-nee, in support of her sister.

Nee-Lah, whose own heart had only just returned to its regular beat, moved to position herself between Kona, Soh-nee and Sey-la, in an effort to end this petty squabbling.

'You have water to secure and a report to make to Torkahn, Kona,' she toned. Nee-Lah spared Kola a quick wink before bustling Kona on his way. Kona withdrew, well aware of the aging Nee-Lah's position within the pod. He was not impressed and quickly moved to squash the female's chatter.

'You are right, old mother,' he toned. 'I must report to the Tor of what has occurred here. But first we must see if these cold-bloods are still with us,' he called importantly. Eyeing his son closely, Kona's deep tone sent Kola a chill warning.

'We will discuss your failure later, Kola.'

Moving away from the group of pining females' Kona swam slowly, his eyes unmoving. Feeling Sorryl's disapproving eye watching him, Kona swam off to patrol the bay just in case the remaining Cold-bloods were unwise enough to be still lingering nearby. Watching Kona as he swam from his sight, Torryn did not like the cold way that Kona had studied him. As Kona swam away he was aware that Torryn was watching him. Meeting Kona's eye for a brief instant, Torryn made sure that he did not dare to blink, sensing that Kona should not be trusted. Kona returned Torryn's stare with a dark eye.

There was something about the Tor's youngest son that disturbed him. He knew that he had better be doubly sure from now on, as to the continued care and protection of the Tor's dam and his youngest son. At least for the moment. Kona's mind continued to work as he conjured the beginnings of a plan. He would now return to Torkahn to inform him of the attack, and of Kola's actions in preventing what could so easily have ended in tragedy.

With Kona safely out of a tones range, and relieved that Torryn had somehow managed to survive, and to kill several cold-bloods, Sorryl shared her feelings with those nearest to her.

'It is no wonder why that bull swims alone, 'piped Sorryl.

'A big tone and a bully,' called Soh-nee in agreement.

'Enough of this empty toning,' called Nee-Lah in concern. She had never had to swim between members of her own pod before. Kona had overstepped his responsibility. She sensed a dark feeling swimming within Kona. Pushing this dark tide of thought to the back of her mind, she swam to comfort a still fretting Torney and Nayla. Catching Torryn watching her, Nee-Lah had a strong sense that Torryn, too, had sensed something in Kona's spirit.

Kola moved slowly through the sea. He swam at a loss to explain just how this number of Mako had come to such a sudden end? He knew deep within himself that he had only accounted for one of these deaths. Surely Torryn could not have slain three of these crooked-teeth all on his own? Torryn had suffered a wound, and indeed he was the son of the Tor.

Kola was not at all sure what had happened. Swimming slowly on the surface in touch with Sorryl and Torryn, he sucked in lungful's of air before letting it go in a tired sigh. He was relieved. In in his minds-eye he had seen just how close they had all come to near disaster. Had any death or serious injury resulted from the Makos' attack, the responsibility would have been his, and his alone. That Torryn, the Tor's son, had suffered an injury was bad enough. He would now have to face Torkahn to explain his how and why Torryn had been hurt, and how he had permitted these killer's entry into the bay.

Zaar and his remaining followers swam in shock at what had happened. Swimming slowly because he had suffered a staggering blow, the pain still grasped his flank as Zaar stared wide-eyed and unblinking into the green murk in front of him. He was convinced that the others had let him down. Beaten by a pup and a weakened group of females. But something else troubled him. He could not explain how the lone sentry they had passed when entering the bay could have moved so quickly to intercept them? To lose so many of their number in so short a time, made no sense, and surely that lone bull could not move as swiftly, and fight as bravely as if they were facing two such fish? Zaar sensed something. It was a feeling that left him feeling more than a little confused. A sense that he was somehow not swimming alone in the sea. He shook himself. His attack had failed and that was all that mattered to him. With his stomach rumbling, his thoughts once again returned to the hunting of his prey, and of filling his empty belly. He had lived to hunt and kill another day. Those that had not were not his concern.

By the time Kona had made half of the long swim back toward the last known position of the pod, Torkahn had already re-grouped and was now leading the hunt back toward Shelter Bay at the best possible speed. Torkahn sensed Kona's return long before Kona's shadow emerged from the afternoon gloom of the sea.

'I see you, Kona,' Torkahn toned expectantly. 'What news have you of the females' and the young?' Moving silently through the sea Kona passed down Torkahn's flank. With a flick of his powerful tail he swam to join Torkahn, Rally and Daks, who were each swimming at a brisk pace through the sea.

Kona spared himself from greeting the Tor's two elder sons, sensing the serious tone of Torkahn's demanding greeting.

'The females are safe, Tor,' toned Kona, 'as are the young.' 'But,' replied Torkahn, his deep tone echoing flatly and without emotion. Kona hesitated, but only very briefly before giving tone to his reply. 'Your intuition was correct, Tor.' Kona found that he could not meet Torkahn's eye. Instead he bowed his head into the on-coming sea, in what he hoped Torkahn would see as a show of his respect and sincerity.

'And? Share your tone, Kon-neh-nah,' Torkahn ordered, his call sounding sharp and demanding.

'A cold-blood raiding party mounted an attack on the nursing pod, Tor. The attack was repulsed by the actions of both Kola and myself,' toned Kona with pride. 'Four cold-bloods are no more, my Tor. One being taken by young Torryn-Gah.' Torkahn swam shocked at hearing this piece of news. Taking care in not allowing himself to show it, Torkahn, using several strong thrusts of his tail, moved forward in the sea to give himself some sea-room to think. He himself had placed Kola within easy striking distance, so as to allow Kola to swim into action quickly should the small pod have come under threat. He heard Kona's tone sounding behind him as Kona finished his report. 'Torryn suffered a small wound, Tor. His injury is not great, neither did it effect any vital function.' Kona fell silent. Glancing back toward a silently swimming Rally, Torkahn could sense Rally's own concern for his youngest brother.

'I hear you, and I thank you, Kona. You may return to your station,' toned Torkahn. Kona found that he was trembling as he turned away to swim to his place. Was it fear? Kona feared no living thing. The Tor was large, and Kona had to admit to himself that Torkahn had more than earned his hard-won position as Tor. But Kona, too, demanded respect. He had expected to be invited to continue swimming on in the van to relay the story as he had seen it to Torkahn. But the mighty Tor obviously had other ideas. Dismissing him instead, as if her were an inexperienced yearling.

After a hard swim Torkahn mustered the pod off the mouth of the familiar bay. Rising in the sea he poked out his large, flat tongue and tasted the breeze. The strong winds that had driven the storm of that early morning had dropped away, leaving the surface of the bay flat and calm, with just the occasional roll of the deep Pacific swell dotted with the resting forms of many exhausted seabirds. Sensing his closeness to Sorryl, Torkahn hurriedly gave tone to fresh orders. His urgent call echoing their arrival to the now much relieved nursey group.

Torkahn sent tone for Daks. Watching his middle son arrive through the sea, Torkahn admired the graceful style of Daks' swimming. Daks was so much like his mother. There was much about Daks that reminded Torkahn of his first mate. Daks had been born under a full moon, and like his mother, he swam to a current that only he could feel. Daks had imagination and a good heart. Torkahn loved him dearly.

'I'm with you, father,' called Daks.

'You will patrol the mouth of the bay until you are relieved,' toned Torkahn. 'Yes, father,' returned Daks, his own tone fading rapidly, as his well-muscled tail drove him quickly along to his duty. Torkahn turned his head to lock eyes with Kato. Kato was a close friend of both Daks and Rally, and was of a similar age. The powerfully built bull had joined the Tor-Gah only two cycles before. Kato's arrival had been welcomed by Torkahn, who saw much value in acquiring the loyalty and service of such an obviously capable, skilled and mature hunting bull. Kato's sail rose from beneath the sea shedding a trail of water as he swam to Torkahn's side. Torkahn eyed the strong Orca swimming at his side.

'I see you, Kato. You will patrol to a distance from this point, of three hundred breaths to the south, by two hundred west,' toned Torkahn

'You will keep a sharp sense for the cold-bloods, Kato.' 'And if I sense any?' asked Kato.

'The fish I seek are Mako,' returned Torkahn. 'Do not place yourself in harm's way unnecessarily, Kato. But I want those responsible for this attack,' toned Torkahn, his deep tone leaving Kato in no doubt as to the fate awaiting those who would attempt to harm any son or daughter of the Tor-Gah. 'No creature is safe from these crooked-teeth, Kato,' rumbled Torkahn. Toning a brief farewell to Rally, Kato pointed his jutting snout to the southward, his strong tail driving him forward as he swam to begin his long patrol.

With his mind full of questions yet to be answered, Torkahn led the pod over the bar and into the welcoming shallows of the bay. It was Nee-Lah who first broke the strict silence of the pod. Her tuneful tones calling to the pod that all was well as she swam with Sorryl and Torryn, and the others who were waiting with their young, sheltering at the northern end of the bay.
Torryn squinted into the bright sunlight that painted the sea with a million sparkling stars. He swam under blue sky, the cloud having gone north with the wind, leaving the bay to bathe under a cloudless, late afternoon sky. Sensing Torkahn's arrival, he swam hurriedly toward his father's call. He was filled with the excitement at what had occurred, and of how he had performed in battle! With the light catching Torryn's smooth, black hide, Torkahn could see

that his youngest son appeared to be bursting with energy, as if at any moment he might explode with pride. Catching a brief glimpse of Kola's figure swimming behind the slow-moving females, he quickly passed from Torkahn's view, to melt silently into the gloom beyond. Torkahn recognized that this was not the right moment to address the younger bull. That time would come, and soon enough for both of them. Distracting his thoughts, Torkahn felt his ear echo to Torryn's piercing call.

'I see you, Tor, I see you, Rally,' piped Torryn excitedly.

To Torkahn's ear his youngest son's usually high pitched tone seemed to have changed since only that very morning.

'I hear you, Torryn-Gah. I have heard tone of your heroic exploits in defence of your mother and her sisters.' Slowing his headlong dash toward his father, Torryn angled himself around in the water as he swam to move beneath Torkahn's heavy tail. Swimming happily next to his father, Torryn could not wait to share tone of his fierce encounter with the cold-bloods. He could sense his father eyeing the freshly scarred skin on his back. 'I swim unharmed, father,' toned Torryn.

'I can see that you have been most fortunate, boy,' returned Torkahn. 'I am glad that you were not more seriously injured, my son. Now, you had better tell me how it is that you came to be fighting the crooked-teeth?' Taking a deep breath, Torryn gave tone to his story. Taking special care to tell his father of Kola's gallant actions in swimming to their rescue, he quietly gave tone of Kona's eventual arrival on the scene some minutes later. Torkahn turned his eye. He found and met Nee-Lah's eye for just a moment. The look in the old whale's stare telling him much. Torkahn remained quiet as he swam. He had to admit to himself that Torryn had indeed surprised him. To have the knowledge to track and to then intercept a pack of crazed cold-bloods with their blood up, was rare enough in one so young. Yet the visible proof lay dead on the bottom of the bay for all the pod to see. Dead and motionless as they were, the dead Mako still seemed to weave their web of fear. Their stilled bodies moving slowly, carried by the light bottom current on their last swim, food now for the always busy bottom-dwellers.

Torkahn was not displeased at Torryn's first blooding in combat. He had listened as Torryn shared tone with Rally of the part he had played in the defence of the nursery pod. Rally swam trying to listen, surrounded as he was by a very excitable Torney swimming on one flank, and a very nervous and twitching Nayla swimming close by on the other. No longer would these two piping females have cause to taunt and tease him, thought Torryn to himself. Even Rally, who was floating close by, was enjoying Torryn's very active re-telling of the attack. Torryn enjoyed having Rally's full attention, as his big brother listened to his tone with an exaggerated stare, accompanied by the occasional roll of his friendly eye.

Meeting Torkahn's eye, Rally could sense his father's feelings of relief. The young were safe. Returning his attention to the young calves, Rally realised that they had all been very lucky to survive. Giving Rally a quick wink, Torkahn turned in the sea, leaving Torryn and Rally's excited exchange in favour of seeking out Sorryl, his Sorryl, to share a few quiet moments away from the constant demands of the pod. Torkahn found his mate swimming in slow company with Nee-Lah. Together with Sey-la and Soh-nee, they swam together, enjoying a well-earned rest from the demanding trills of Torney and Nayla.

'I see you Tor,' piped the four females in near musical unison.

'I hear your song, you beauties of the deep,' toned a very sincere Torkahn, as he took care to dip his head in a rare sign of respect and greeting. There was only one tuneful tone that Torkahn strained his ear to catch.

'I hear your tone, Sorryl,' he called. 'I would have you swim with me.' He watched as his graceful mate broke away from the others to swim in answer to his call.

'I hear you Tor, and I obey,' piped Sorryl, her call sounding in a mischievous and submissive song. 'Please do not call me Tor when we are alone, Sorryl. My time spent with you is the only time that I can truly be myself,' toned Torkahn. Sensing the deep tones of tiredness in her mates call, Sorryl sent a soft tone to her much loved mate. 'I know, Torkahn, and I am sorry,' she crooned. 'It has been a very long day. A day in which I thought I may never see you again.' Their eyes met in a reflection of their shared love and concern for each other. Torkahn felt as if his huge heart might break at the thought of losing one so beautiful to those cruel bringers of death. He felt as if he could swim, lost for an eternity, in the deep pool of Sorryl's shining eye.

'I am glad that I felt your call. I sent Kona back to you immediately,' he toned. 'Please, Torkahn, do not forget, Kola. He fought like the great Tor-Gah himself to defend us,' returned Sorryl in the younger whale's defence. Studying Sorryl's slender figure in silence, Torkahn's next tone echoed his true feelings. 'It was my fault, Sorryl. My stubborn pride placed you all in danger.

If I not told Torryn that I was leaving him in charge of the safety of you all, I would never have risked placing Kola so far from your side.' Sorryl moved to rub Torkahn's side with her rounded snout. 'The fact that you left Kola where you did shows me that you had indeed thought well ahead, Torkahn. You must share tone with Kola. I am sure that he feels that he has in some way failed you.' Torkahn hung in the water, his head dipped low as he considered Sorryl's tone. 'I hear you, Sorryl, and I should hear your sweet tone more often,' toned a grateful Torkahn. 'If you were to see me so often, Tor, who would lead us?' crooned Sorryl. 'Hah!' toned Torkahn, his broad flukes slapping the surface of a smooth sea in an effort to shake free the weight of concern he felt for all those swimming under his care and protection.

'It seems young Torryn, slayer of the cold-blood, would take my place in the van tomorrow!' hooted Torkahn, his arching tail again smashing the surface in playful jest.

'No, please, Tor,' pined Sorryl, 'leave my son with me for just a little while longer.'

'Do not worry so, Sorryl. Torryn's sail is not yet tall enough to cut the waves at the front of my van,' Torkahn assured her. Rising up in the sea to vent and to breathe, before sinking back beneath the waves, Torkahn swam close to his mate to gently rub his snout down the smooth flank of Sorryl's body.

'I must leave you now. Remember my touch until the next time.'

Sorryl watched with a hint of regret as again her mighty bull left her side with a push of his tail flukes.

She listened as the sea echoed to Torkahn's authoritative call, his reassuring tone sounding his orders to his expectant bulls in preparation for the beginning of the evening feed. Straining her eyes in the murky sea, Sorryl watched as Torkahn, her Torkahn, slid from her view, gone now, taken from her by the call of the tide until the time of their next brief meeting.

8.

Torryn learns his place!

With his belly full of fish following the evening hunt, Torkahn circled the bay enjoying the touch of warmth on his skin from a slowly setting sun. As he swam, he studied the scene spread before him, taking the time to search out each member of the pod; identifying them by the white patches of colour set behind each of their shining eyes. With the constant dull blasts of the Tor-Gah's venting, Torkahn found that he enjoyed this time of the day most of all.

With the wild wind spent, the surface of the bay lay dappled and calm. The towering headland on the southward side of the bay casting a long shadow out over the water that lay speckled with the brilliant white of hundreds of feeding terns. As the flaming ball of Rah dropped toward the sea to the west, Torkahn's thoughts turned toward tomorrow, and to the prospect of taking the entire pod back out, and into the wild and untamed blue.

The following morning the first pink touches of the new day were hidden by a thick blanket of mist. The wind hardly a whisper. The still silence of the dawn broken only by the slow sound of venting as if the sea itself were alive. Torkahn's grey outline could just be seen as he moved slowly through the pod, toning in both recognition and encouragement, as he began the muster in readiness for their leaving the always welcomed safety and familiarity of Shelter Bay.

Kato had returned early in the darkened hours before dawn. His muscled frame breaking the surface next to Torkahn, while at the same time he expelled a deep blast of air from his blowhole. To Torkahn it sounded like a mighty sigh, the sure sign of a prolonged swim.

'You have travelled well, Kato. I was not expecting you until the rise of Rah. What have you seen?' toned Torkahn.

'Oh, Tor, I have swum as you directed but the blue gave no sign of the surviving cold-bloods that you seek,' returned Kato, his head bowed in regret.

'The blue is peaceful and lies undisturbed.'

'A most disappointing outcome,' returned Torkahn.

'But not unexpected, father. These fish will have run deep and swiftly,' toned Rally, who had been patiently listening to Kato's unhurried report while swimming close at his father's side.

'You are right, Rah-leh-lah. But mark my tone well. We shall meet with these cold-bloods again, and then the tide will turn!' barked Torkahn, his ominous tone echoing his threat to the very sea itself.

Taking up his position Torkahn swam leading the pod out over the sand bar toward the freedom of the open sea. Moving through the ghostly white veil that hung just above the surface of the water, Torkahn was joined by Rally and the usually silent Kona, as he ordered Kato to his rest after his return from his long patrol. Watching Kato, Torkahn's thoughts turned to Daks. Earlier that morning he had sent Daks ahead scouting to the north east. They would meet up later in the day. Slowly the pod moved into position, the females,' safe in the huddled security afforded by the middle of the pod, with the young swimming close to their mothers' sides swam in readiness through the blanketing mist.

Torryn could be found swimming in close company between Nee-Lah and Sorryl. He had fidgeted and slapped his tail all that previous night as the pod had kept up its slow night swim round the bay for what would be the last time for many tides. For him, the dawn could not come quickly enough! Rising up from beneath the surface he exhaled old air in a loud huff, before greedily sucking in a fresh breath.

He could taste the chill freshness of the dawn. The high outlines of the cliffs just visible through the all enshrouding mist. The shadowy crags lined with the small white bodies of the nesting terns. The glimpses of the sky through the now thinning veil of mist, giving him a sight of that other blue world that existed far above his head.

To interrupt his early morning day dreaming he felt a blast of air as the water erupted alongside of him. Shouldering poor Nee-Lah from her position, Rally's head and sail appeared next to his younger brother, his blowhole quivering as he took in a strong breath. 'I bring you the greetings of a new tide, little brother!' toned Rally, to a very surprised Torryn. 'I see you too, Nee-Lah, and Sorryl,' toned Rally. 'May the good fortunes of a new hunt fill your bellies this day.' Torryn watched as Nee-Lah gave Rally a playful nudge.

'I hear you, Rah-leh-lah,' she piped. 'You have caused me to suffer the embarrassment of losing several tail strokes thanks to your play. You should show more respect to your elders and betters,' she toned. Nee-Lah did her best to sound disapproving. Rally knew that he had done wrong. 'You have my humblest of apologies, second mother. I thought yours was the tail of one of the younger dams. Surely I was not mistaken?' he toned. 'I hear you, Rally, returned Nee-Lah, never quite knowing from where next the fun loving Rally would appear. 'If you are having such difficulty identifying tails, then surely this pod should be worried for its short-sighted future,' she teased. Sorryl, too, had sensed Rally's approach, her motherly instincts sending her a strong message of what as about to come. Rally met her eye with his own own before sharing tone.

'Torryn is to accompany me to take a position in the van,' he toned. Thinking that he must have misheard his elder brother, Torryn shook his head, feeling that perhaps he had seaweed caught in his ears! Surely he was not yet ready to take up his position swimming at the head of the pod?

'Come, Torryn-Gah,' toned Rally, 'we keep the Tor waiting.'

'Oh, we can't have that, now, can we. They must all be losing their sight up there if they have to call in one so young to lead the van!' called Nee-Lah cheekily. With barely the time to farewell his mother and Nee-Lah, Torryn felt himself being half carried, half pushed, in a cloud of trailing foam and wake toward the front of the pod, and to the taste of the cool open sea that stretched invitingly ahead of him.

Appearing together, Rally and Torryn broke water to swim in the clear seaway on Torkahn's right flank. Torryn was elated to be at last able to get a taste of the deep sea. In fact, the sea did taste different out here, he thought to himself. Moving effortlessly through the bluish green ocean, he enjoyed the feeling of the cool caress of the sea flowing over his sleek body. With each new breath he took, he found his senses showered with the enticing scents and tastes of his hazy new world.

With his back shimmering to the steady stream of white water running across his broad flanks, Torkahn dipped beneath the surface to briefly lock eyes with Torryn. To Torryn's ear his father's muted tone sounded soft and welcoming.

'Do not fear, young one. I thought that you may enjoy a taste of the blue up here with the bulls.' Kato's deep throated rumble echoed Torkahn's tone, as he dropped down to swim under Torryn, giving him a gentle nudge with his wide nose.

'It is time for you to swim away from those females' who would all spoil you so,' toned Rally, his blurred form obscured from Torryn's view by Kato's slow return to the surface. Offering his own hesitant greetings, Torryn found himself distracted by the cool touch of the unbroken ocean stretching out endlessly ahead. Sensing his youngest son's eagerness and excitement to be on the swim, Torkahn watched as Torryn gave strength to his tail and increased his pace. Rally met Kato's eye to give his friend a wink. Torryn's nose was pulling slowly ahead of that of his Tor. Torkahn caught Rally's eye as he, too, continued to keep a half an eye on Torryn's progress through the sea.

'I see you, Torryn-Gah,' toned Rally. 'I fear it is not good manners to allow your nose to appear swimming ahead of that of your Tor.' Realising his error, Torryn rested his tail to allow himself to drop back in the sea, swimming to keep better station with his father, his ears echoing to his father's deep tone.

'One day you will earn the right to swim at the head of your own pod, Torryn-Gah. Until that day comes, your tail should never be seen waving in front of my van. Something else to remember, thought Torryn to himself. He knew now that he had a lot to learn before he could earn his true place as a trusted member of the van, as Kato, Kona, Daks and Rally were.

Torkahn sensed that his youngest son was struggling to understand the meaning of such things. Perhaps Torney and Nayla were right after all, Torryn thought to himself. Maybe I am just not ready yet. 'Raise your tail, Torryn-Gah!' Torkahn's tone chimed in his ear. What have I done now? Torryn thought to himself. More rules? But he was surprised! His father's tone carried with it news that was unbelievable! 'You will spend two hundred breaths of each new day swimming with the van, Torryn. You will watch, listen and learn. You will accompany each hunt as the shadow of any bull that I may choose to direct to this task,' toned Torkahn. Not daring to break his father's tone, Torryn swam in respectful silence. He felt higher than the highest king tide at hearing this piece of unexpected news. At last he would have the opportunity to swim ahead of the pod, taking his own chances out there in the blue. Torryn felt as if he was swimming in a trance. 'Now return to your mother and tell her of my decision,' Torkahn ordered. 'If you can survive that, then you can survive anything.' The others whistled and slapped the surface with the flats of their tails on hearing Torkahn's tone. Torryn didn't understand. All he wanted to do was swim!

As the pod formed up, each whale swam to take their positions for the long swim ahead. Rally stilled himself in the water. Holding his body rigid, he felt his senses tingle to a faint presence in the sea. He held his tone, unsure as to just what it was that he was feeling. He could not sense from which direction this feeling came, or why. It was as if whatever it was, was all around them. Trying to shake off the feeling, he imagined that perhaps it had been just the movement of the sea. If there was a presence out there watching the progress of the pod, then he could sense no living threat. The one single feeling that left him feeling most uneasy, was that whatever this presence was, it was a sense that he felt that he should somehow recognize. A feeling as familiar to him, as it was unfamiliar.

Sending strength to his tail, he swam to catch his father and to take up his position on the swim. Since there was no visible threat to the pod that he could detect, he chose to remain silent, and to not share tone of his feelings with Torkahn. Satisfied with his decision, he moved through the sea, his mind already swimming head of the pod as he greedily thought of the large fish that would soon be sliding down his gullet.

Swimming close to Rally's solid flank, Torryn kept up the rhythm of the pace with each solid thrust of his tail. He could hear his mother swimming several lengths behind in the company of Nee-Lah, Sey-la and Soh-nee. He could hear the reassuring tones of Nee-Lah's singing echoing all round them. Turning back his eye, he caught sight of Torney and Nayla, who were swimming beside Nee-Lah, leaping and playing in her wake. He watched as they twisted and turned, and rose and fell in the water like feathers caught in a breeze. Not even their close encounter with Zaar and his henchmen had made Torney and Nayla any more careful or considerate of others, he thought. He could not wait to show them his tail, if only for a few short breaths.

He had quite mistakenly thought that their teasing and torment would stop following his recent killing of a cold-blood, now but a distant memory and a lesson well-learned. Having grown tired of hearing their taunts as they playfully teased him about his at last being able to swim with the bulls, Torryn swam sure that one day, in the not too distant future, that he would have his own back on his two noisy and sometimes tiresome companions.   Feeling his ear buzz to a familiar tone, Torryn instantly recognized his friend Kola's call. With his ear sounding to Rally's reply, Torryn searched the water around him for Kola's form, locating him swimming alongside the shadowed and silent shape of his hard toned father, Kona.

'I see you, Kona,' toned Rally. Torryn listened, but there was no reply from the silently swimming Kona. Watching Kona as he continued to swim, his tail pushing his length through the sea at an easy pace, Torryn met Kona's eye for just a split second before Kona lifted his head in his slow climb upward to catch his next breath. Torryn felt the still fresh scar on his back give a slight twinge. Waiting until they had moved a safe distance from Kona and Kola, Torryn swam close to Rally, his tone sounding tense and whispered. 'Why does Kona fail to return our greetings this morning, Rally?'

Taken by surprise at hearing such a question from his young brother, Rally rolled his eye to glance back to make eye contact with Torryn.

'It does not do to ask an elder why he does, What he does, Torryn,' Rally toned. 'Kona is a bull of the Tor-Gah, and as such, he does not have to do anything other than to follow the order and the direction of the Tor.' Torryn listened and considered Rally's tone before making his reply.

'I'm glad Kona is not my father,' he toned. 'When I am near him the mark left on my back by the cold-blood tingles strangely.'

'Perhaps it is not yet properly healed,' returned Rally, as he swam to gently nudge his young brother with his snout. 'Do not share tone of this with the Tor,' warned Rally, his tone set in a deep echo.

'It is not our place to give tone to such things, Torryn.' Torryn understood his brother and replied in almost a whisper, 'I hear you, Rally.'

'As you should, little brother,' Rally answered, Satisfied that Torryn had understood his warning. Studying his younger brother closely, Rally found himself wondering about just it was that could be eating at Kona. Thinking of Kola, and considering Torryn's feelings about Kona, Rally had learned that he must not judge the actions of his elders. Kola was a fine young whale. Strong, clever and eager to please the Tor

Arriving at the head of the pod, Torryn felt his ears ring to his father's call of greeting. 'I trust that you are well nourished and well rested, Torryn,' greeted Torkahn. 'I am feeling fit and ready to swim to the hunt,' returned Torryn with great enthusiasm.

'Are you indeed?' toned Torkahn, eyeing his youngest son closely with a friendly eye.

'Then perhaps it is high time that you were given the opportunity to test your tail?'

Torryn was too stunned to reply. Giving Rally a wink, Torkahn gave tone to Torryn as he would one of his bulls.

'You will swim ready to join the hunt today, Torryn-Gah. You will swim in the company of a bull of my choosing. You will swim to his tone,' directed Torkahn. 'There, now, you have what you wished.' Rally swam silently not wishing to disturb Torryn's special moment with their father. Torryn felt as if he was floating on a bed of bubbles with the excitement of his father's decision. 'Leave me now, Torryn. Rally will answer any questions you may have, and I am sure that you have many,' toned Torkahn, looking to Rally.

Swimming to guide Torryn back toward the middle of the pod, Rally caught his father's last tone. 'On your way, Rally, please locate Kola, and tell him to join me.'

Rally met Torryn's eye at hearing Kola's name. Sensing that his father wished to swim alone, Rally pushed Torryn back in the direction of the trailing pod.

'We must find, Kola,' toned Rally. Torryn wondered how it would go for his friend in front of his father. The Tor was large, and even Torryn found that his father's moods often echoed the moods of the sea itself. Smooth and calm one moment, but dark and stormy the next.

'Do not worry for Kola, Torryn. Kola's tail may be lowered, but you and I both know that father swims a straight course. Kola will be given a fair hearing,' toned Rally. Picking out the blurred form of Kola as they swam, Rally offered his greeting before informing Kola of the Tor's not unexpected request. Catching Kola's eye, Torryn gave him a heads-up gesture as he swam by.

'See you on the hunt, Kola,' he called. Watching Rally and Torryn disappear into the murk, Kola tried to imagine what lay in store for him in the presence of his all-seeing and all-knowing Tor.

As he swam he remembered his father's tone of the night before. Be on your guard when you are before the Tor, his father had warned. You did everything that was expected of you, Kola, and more. With his father's stern tone still echoing in his head, Kola left his position on the landward side of the pod. Swimming with an added haste, he had no time to seek out and greet others.

Instead, as was expected of him, he swam obediently to the head of the steadily moving pod, where Torkahn swam in wait for Kola's arrival. Having once been Kola's age himself, Torkahn had not forgotten his own feelings when he too had been summoned to swim at his Tor's side. Swimming alone some distance ahead of the pod, Torkahn sensed Kola's arrival, sending a reassuring greeting to the young and visibly nervous Kola.

'I see you, Koh-leh-lah,' Torkahn called.

'I hear you, Tor, and I answer your call,' Kola toned obediently.

Eyeing the young whale swimming at his side, Torkahn could sense Kola's nervousness. He watched as Kola swam in an awkward crawl, almost as if the younger whale was holding his breath. Kola swam with a stiff tail, his head held rigidly still as he dived, and then surfaced, some half a length back from Torkahn's eye. Torkahn relaxed his tone. 'Swim with me for a few breaths, Kola.' Letting go of his breath, Kola relaxed visibly in the sea at hearing Torkahn's calmly delivered invitation. Using several extra thrusts of his tail, Kola swam to draw level with Torkahn's dark eye. Looking up, Kola rested his eye on the Tor's awesome sail. He imagined Torkahn's towering sail must reach to the very sky itself. Breaking the silence between them, Torkahn at last gave tone to his feelings.

'I thought it time that we shared tone of your action in defence of the nursery pod.' Kola felt a sinking feeling in his empty stomach. He held his breath, daring himself not to breathe, as he listened obediently for what was to come.

'Your actions at the mouth of the bay placed both the females' and the young in your charge in peril, Kola,' boomed Torkahn. Torkahn knew that his manner was harsh, but the young Orca had to hear it. Kola, just like himself, had to be made to learn from his own mistakes.

'I left you with strict instructions to patrol and cover the entry to the bay in my absence,' continued Torkahn. All Kola could manage as he am in his Tor's shadow was a quiet, 'I hear you, Tor.' Torkahn continued. 'Through your own negligence, you allowed the safe passage of the cold-bloods into a known sanctuary of the Tor-Gah.' Torkahn swam in silence, allowing his call to sink in before he continued. 'However, your actions upon hearing the calls of your charges was rapid and what is expected of a bull of this pod, Kola.'

Kola felt his spirits take a brief lift as he continued to listen to the deep tone of his Tor.

'You then failed to detect the arrival of Kona during your engagement with the cold-bloods,' toned Torkahn. 'I hear you, Tor,' returned Kola, dropping his head in shame. Eyeing the young bull swimming head down and obediently at his flank, Torkahn's mind echoed to his memory of

Sorryl's kindly tone in support of the young whale swimming at his side. Kola continued to listen intently as Torkahn went on to give tone to his own small confession. 'I myself, must take some of the blame for what might have occurred, Kola. It was I who ordered you to patrol the mouth of the bay, was it not?'
Allowing his tone to die in the sea, Torkahn waited a half breath before continuing. 'Instead, Kola, I should have ordered you to remain swimming in close protection of the females' and their young. I did this so that Torryn might have the briefest taste of responsibility, Kola, but I was wrong to do so!'

Kola could hardly believe his senses. The Tor himself was sharing in a portion of the blame. 'But you are not without fault, Kola,' toned Torkahn. 'Neither of us are. When you are securing or closing off an area, you should not patrol from one fixed point to another, and never on a straight course.'
Kola listened intently, feeling now as if at last things may be returning to normal for him. Torkahn continued, his tone sounding calm as he added some much needed advice. 'You should always swim a patrol in a circular pattern between two points, Kola. It provides you with the chance to sound more effectively should you need to do so. Take this as a shared lesson well-

learned, Kola, and one day you will earn your place swimming in my van.'

Having heard and understood Torkahn's message, Kola toned his grateful understanding to the dark shape swimming at his side. 'I shall be looking to you, Kola,' toned Torkahn, an expectant growl sounding in his authoritative call. 'Now leave me and return to your position, for I have much to think about.' Kola did not have to be told twice! Toning his grateful salute, and by dropping one flipper and raising another, Kola was soon gone from sight. Torkahn swam pleased that Kola had taken both his advice and his warning well. He liked Kola. He swam in hope that the young whale was swimming lighter in the sea following their brief time together. For Torkahn this was a day neither he, or young Kola, would quickly forget. The beginnings of a new trust between them had begun, carried as it was on the fresh current of an incoming tide.

9.
To the hunter go the spoils.

The last rays of the slowly setting sun painted the clouds floating on the western horizon a brilliant shade of pink. Swimming to join his father at the head of the pod, Rally took up his place swimming on Torkahn's flank, while Torryn swam happily between the two solid walls of his father, and the tall sailed shape of Kato, who loomed swimming at a relaxed pace on the other. 'I see you, Tor,' toned Rally. 'I trust that all went well between you and Kola?'
Turning his eye upon his eldest son, Torkahn eyed Rally with a silent stare.

'I have shared tone with Kola,' returned Torkahn.

'Then all is well, Tor?' toned Rally, not wishing to press his father on this most delicate subject.

'You may swim assured that all is as it should be, my son,' returned Torkahn. 'I hear you, Tor,' returned Rally. Watching Torkahn rise and fall in the sea, Rally could see that his father swam deep in thought. Rally was beginning to come to understand that leading a pod was an awesome

Responsibility, and no easy task.

As the Tor's eldest son, Rally swam in the certain knowledge that one day in the distant future, he would be swimming in his father's place as head of the pod. He hoped that such a day was still a long time off, as he knew that he still had much to learn before he could take his place swimming and leading others as Torkahn did. For the present, Rally was content to swim at his father's side, where he could watch and learn.

As the lowering sun sank slowly into the sea on the western horizon, Rally remained swimming with his father in the dim light of the gathering dusk. As the sun finally disappeared to be swallowed by the blue, the evening sky came alive with a million stars.

Moving at a relaxed pace through the sea, Torkahn noticed Torryn taking an interest in the night sky. A million tiny pin-pricks of light seemed to Torryn to be dancing about just above his head. Dipping beneath the sea he finally gave in to his wary muscles. Sensing that Torryn was swimming more asleep than awake, Torkahn ordered Rally to escort Torryn to his mother's side. 'You have done well, today, Torryn-Gah. I am proud of you. But now it is time to rest your tail, young one. Return to your mother now, Torryn. You must rest, for tomorrow is another day.'

As reluctant as he was to leave his father's side, Torryn felt so tired that he could hardly wave his tail. 'Tomorrow?' he piped, his flat tone echoing his tiredness.

'Will be soon enough,' toned Torkahn. 'Go with Rally, Torryn. I shall swim to you when the moon rises.' Torryn had grown to enjoy his father's visits over the dark-time. Each night, Torkahn would return to find Sorryl and Torryn as he expected, swimming in their usual places within the pod. Torkahn would swim with Torryn for a few breaths, enjoying his time spent answering his newest son's endless current of questions; the answers to which Torryn absorbed like a thirsty sea-sponge. Each evening, as the clouds permitted, Torkahn gave tone to Torryn of the story behind each different set of stars and their meaning to Orca lore, as he had done with both Rally and Daks, before him.

Appearing as he always did swimming in the blue hue of the climbing moon, Torkahn found Torryn resting in his place between Nee-Lah and Sorryl, as they cradled him between them in the sea. Feeling Torkahn's sleek body rub slowly along her own, Sorryl toned her pleasure at Torkahn's return to her.

'I see you, my Tor,' she sang in a whisper that to Torkahn sounded like the breaking of a tiny wave.

'And I hear you, Sorryl, queen of the blue,' hummed Torkahn in greeting.

'Torryn grows stronger with the passing of each moon,' called Sorryl. Her mournful tone giving sound to her worried concern for the active life of her only son. 'It is so,' returned Torkahn. 'He takes to his new responsibilities well. The passing of several moons will soon see Torryn taking a more active part in the life of the pod.' Sorryl swam in silent thought before releasing her next tone. 'But he is still so young, Torkahn. I fear that he will leave my side too soon, and my little Torryn will be lost to me forever.' Torkahn heard and understood his mate's soulful echo of concern.

Expelling air in a loud huff, Torkahn sank below the waves, his tone sounding the sincere feelings behind his reply.

'I hear you, Sorryl. Why do you address me this way?' he toned.

'Have I done wrong?' returned Sorryl.

'No,' toned Torkahn. 'You are who you are, Soh-reh-lah, just as Torryn is who he is. His place is at my side. His life, just like yours and my own, belong to the pod. You must come to accept this, Sorryl.' Deep inside herself Sorryl knew that her mate gave tone to the truth. She only wished to protect and to shield her son, but she also knew that Torryn was, in his own unique way, special; different somehow, in a way that she did not yet fully understand.

Swimming side by side, Sorryl and Torkahn swam matching breath for breath, for what seemed to Torkahn, all too short a time.

Soon it would be time for him to swim in answer to the call of his van, to take charge of the morning muster. With a last run up the slim line of Sorryl's flank with his nose, Torkahn slid past Sorryl's eye, his deep-set tone already directing the members of his family to the fresh and challenging rewards of a new days hunt.

Torryn was wide awake. He had rested well over the dark time, when he had at last been able to let his thoughts go with the tide, where he dreamed of joining the hunt on the following dawn. With the rising of the sun he could hear the usual far off chorus of the flocks of feeding seabirds. To his eye, the surface of the sea appeared as flat and as calm as it had been in many a day's swim. Dropping his tail he rose in the water to test the air with his fat, pink tongue, as he had watched Torkahn do. The new light of day was dimmed by a thick bank of mist that again hovered over the calm of the water.

Catching sight of Torkahn, who swam as a ghostly grey outline through the sea, he followed his father's shadow as his tall sail moved through the pod, the distinct sound of his father's tone offering each member of his family his usual enthusiastic morning greetings that echoed throughout the sea.

Sighting Torryn hanging tail down in the sea, Torkahn could hardly believe how quickly Torryn had grown from the small calf whose untimely arrival had surprised them all so, only a few short months before. Torkahn had sensed that Torryn was watching him. Was Torryn ready to take on the demands of a full day's swimming? He wondered. Despite Sorryl's tones of concern, Torkahn swam sure that Torryn swam more than ready to accompany them on their journey. Waving his tail, Torryn pushed himself through the mist covered sea towards his father, unsure as to whether or not he should disturb him at such a peaceful time.

'Good dawning to you, my son,' hummed Torkahn in greeting.

'And how does your tail feel today, Torryn-Gah?' Torryn wriggled his tail and rolled over, forgetting as he did so, to close his blowhole. Rolling right over in the sea, he felt the water flow down his blowhole, the water making him splutter and snort as he struggled to right himself and clear his airway.

'My tail feels fine, father,' he spluttered. 'I am ready to swim with the hunt as you promised. I know that I can swim to match the pace, father. Mother may not believe it, but I know that I can,' he called.

Rising up in the mist covered water with his nose pointing straight up toward the sky; a sky that lay hidden above the heavy blanket of sea-mist, Torkahn poked out his tongue revealing a glimpse of his rows of sharp teeth. Torkahn was tasting the breeze. Feeling the strength and direction of the faint breeze that was already springing up as the day began, Torkhan sank back beneath the sea to send tone to Torryn's waiting ear.

'Are you sure that you are ready, Torryn? To swim every day at an increased pace takes discipline and strength. Once you take on the responsibility of swimming to the pace, there is no going back. When we return to the open sea you must learn to swim as one with the pod, my son. Every move you make has an effect on each of those you swim with. You must swim to my tone, and no other, Torryn. It is important you do this. If you do not, then you are placing not only yourself in grave danger, but also the lives of all of those who swim with you.'

'I'm ready, father,' piped Torryn. Torkahn watched as Torryn arched his back in the sea to give more height to his still stubby sail. 'Very well, Torryn-Gah. You shall have your chance to test your tail, if you are sure that you can swim to my tone,' called Torkahn.

'You mean I can swim with you and the others,

father?' toned Torryn in disbelief! 'Yes, Torryn. Now I must see to the hunt. I will send tone for you soon. Listen for my call when it comes,' toned Torkahn. Watching his father disappear through the early morning mist, Torryn could hardly believe his ears. At last he was to join in the hunt!

Having reached his first half cycle in age, Torryn felt that his sail had filled out and jutted, he was sure, at least another half-fluke in height. The well exercised muscles in his tail had grown stronger and more defined; the added weight he had gained in his thick insulating fat coming from the goodness of his mother's milk.

With Nee-Lah's help, Sorryl had been trying to wean Torryn from his over-attraction to her thick, creamy milk. Each time he had tried to sneak in and under Sorryl to grab an easy snack, Nee-Lah was always there with her searching snout, which she used to push him firmly, but gently away. With the free nourishment of his mother so cruelly reduced, Torryn discovered that hunting was now a daily necessity, especially if he was going to continue to grow!

More important than that, was that he did not enjoy feeling empty. His rumbling stomach had developed a language all of its own. The strange noises it made seemed to come just as he was again feeling the aching pangs of hunger. How could he think about food at a time like this? He was far too excited at the prospect of swimming to the hunt!

Floating in the mist covered sea, Torryn listened intently for his father's call. He was eager to be swimming in the company of the other bulls as is father had promised. On his return from entertaining the young females, Rally noticed Torryn impatiently waving his tail. At last the call came. Torryn felt his ears echo to an excited current of sound. Rally, too, heard their fathers' searching call. 'You are to swim with the hunt today, Torryn-Gah!' called Rally excitedly. Lowering his head, Rally pushed Torryn forward in the sea. 'Come, Torryn. We dare not keep the Tor waiting on such a perfect morning for the hunt.' Torryn found that he could not form a tone in his head such was his excitement. He was to join the hunt at last. Trying to hide his sense of excitement as he trailed in Rally's wake, Torryn could see the blurred shapes of Daks, Kato and Kola, each swimming in tight circles, as they playfully jostled each other in the sea. He sensed the usually solitary figure of Kona, who he could see lurking on the outskirts of the hunting pack, his shadow showing pale through the low hanging sea-mist. Hearing Torkahn's orders as he detailed Rally and Kola to remain behind to protect the females and their young, Torryn watched as both Rally and Kola swam to their allotted duty, sad that they could not all swim together on this, his special day. Before he could sound his feelings, he heard his father's tone calling him to the hunt.

'This morning you join the hunt, Torryn!' boomed Torkahn. 'You will swim with Kato this day. Mind you learn his ways, Torryn, and remember to stay close to his tail.' Sensing Kato appear solid and reassuring swimming at his Side, Torryn's ears rang to the many tones and echoes of farewell as Torkahn led the trailing pack to the hunt. As was his habit, Torkahn used his tones sparingly. As the bulls fanned out in front of their Tor, Torryn swam as instructed, hugging in close to Kato's flank.

'I have the eyes of the Tor upon me this day,' toned Kato to Torryn. His base echo sending an unmistakable warning to Torryn's ear.

'I hear you, Kato. Do not worry, I shall not let you down,' returned Torryn.

'See that you do not, young Torryn-Gah,' toned Kato, giving Torryn a quick wink. Hugging in close to Kato's flank, and keeping his mind fixed firmly on matching the energetic pace being set for him by the more powerful and broad tailed Kato, together they swam to the hunt.

Following Kato through the sea, Torryn soon found the shimmering form of their morning breakfast as it appeared through the early morning gloom of the sea. The swirling mass of Mackerel making a wonderful visual display; the early morning light bouncing off thousands of lashing bodies. Torryn watched in awe as the huge ball of silvery fish seemed to shrink and then grow, as the now panicked school Feeling his stomach close to bursting with the amount of Mackerel he had swallowed, Torryn swam slowly, his muscles feeling the strain of the very hectic work required when swimming to the hunt.

With feeding complete, the remains of the Mackerel were allowed to swim on, leaving the much reduced school to escape into the shadows. The larger fish swam to be lost in the sea, as even larger fish, with dark unblinking eyes, cruised in to see what could be had in the way of an easy meal. Torryn's eye caught the far off glint of the sun's rays catching a fleeting form. Cold-bloods! He felt the twinge of his scar sending him its message to swim aware. Feeling a shiver run up his spine, his ears filled with Kato's reassuring yet hurried tone, calling for him to swim and catch him up. Not wishing to be left alone for too long in his wild new world, he sent strength to his tail to swim quickly after Kato, his eyes fastened onto the security offered by Kato's waving tail.

Well-satisfied with their morning's work, Torkahn swam pleased that all those involved had performed well. Seeing Torryn keeping the pace swimming close to Kato's flank had also pleased him. Torryn had proven himself more than capable of being able to keep up with the strenuous chase of the hunt.

Changing his heading in the water, Torkahn lead the pod away from the mist bound land and the familiar safety of Shelter Bay, and out into the open sea. Swimming in company with his mother and Nee-Lah, Torryn helped make their long swim more interesting, by sharing his excited stories of his recent experiences while swimming on the hunt. Nee-Lah listened attentively to Torryn's active description of his exciting morning spent swimming with Kato. As she listened and shared in Torryn's excitement, she noticed that Sorryl had closed her eyes. Knowing Sorryl as she did, the wise Nee-Lah had sensed that Sorryl was swimming against the strong currents of thought that were flooding her mind. Opening her eyes, Sorryl saw Nee-Lah's soft eye watching her. Feeling that Sorryl could benefit from her advice, Nee-Lah sent tone to Torryn. 'Thank you for your most interesting account of the hunt,' Nee-Lah toned kindly. 'You must leave us for a while, Torryn. I must share tone with your mother.' Sensing that Nee-Lah wished to discuss things that were not for his ears, Torryn swam off in search of Torney and Nayla.

Swimming to share water with Sorryl, Nee-Lah gave gentle tone to her thoughts, 'You are unhappy with Torkahn's recent decision to to allow Torryn more freedom outside of your control?' Nee-Lah watched Sorryl as finally the flood of Sorryl's feelings became too much for the new mother to hold back any longer.

'Oh, Nee-Lah, it is true that I do worry so for Torryn's future. He is of my blood. How can I allow him to leave my side when I know that if I do, then he will only swim further away from me?' Sorryl pined. Nee-Lah swam slowly as she enjoyed watching the dimmed reflection of the sun's rays dancing in reflection on Sorryl's flanks. Hearing and understanding the reasons behind Sorryl's concerns, Nee-Lah shared her next tone with Sorryl.

'All mothers' feel as you do, my dear. You wish to protect Torryn. To make sure that he learns to recognize all of the dangers in the sea, so that he will be prepared. You are right to feel as you do. But you must have confidence in Torkahn's ability to share your concerns. What Torkahn does, he does for the good of us all. He would never ask Torryn to do something that was beyond his abilities, or that would place Torryn in deliberate danger. Torkahn has raised two fine sons over many moons, my dear. You must learn to place your trust in Torkahn, and place your faith in his tone.'

'I hear you, Nee-Lah and I thank you for allowing me to fill your ear with my silly fears,' toned Sorryl.

'Have no fear, Sorryl. In time, Torryn will grow

to become a large and handsome bull just like his father.' Feeling relieved that she had shared her concerns with the wise Nee-Lah, Sorryl sensed that Nee-Lah gave tone to the truth.

'Torryn will always return to you, Sorryl. As sure as the sun rises in the east, he will never be far from your side. Behind her shining eye Nee-Lah swam in the secret knowledge that Torryn was a chosen one. For her, Torryn was special; blessed and protected by the spirits of the great blue. Nee-Lah knew, too, that this was not the time to share tone of such things with Sorryl, sensing that Sorryl still worried and fretted about the future of her first born calf.

All too soon Daks' friendly tone could be heard as his familiar form emerged through the sea. Sensing that Sorryl knew that her young son's time spent swimming with her was nearing an end, Nee-Lah shifted in the sea to place herself closer to Sorryl. Sorryl felt her heart sink like a stone as her ear caught Daks' call.

'Hello, second mother,' tooted Daks, as he cruised in close to Sorryl.

'I hear you, Daks,' pined Sorryl in return, as she watched Daks glide by using strong, steady strokes of his tail.

Sensing Sorryl's discomfort, and seeing Nee-Lah's brief signal for him to hurry on, Daks remained silent as he continued on his way to seek out Torryn. He found Torryn swimming in the excited company of the always noisy Torney and Nayla. The sea echoing to their playful calls. Torney and Nayla always looked forward to Daks' brief visits. Torryn's ears quivered with the ear splitting tones of his two young companions as they each made the most of Daks' playful appearance. Torryn swam in impatient circles as Daks tried to swim clear of his young admirers 'I see you, Torryn,' he toned. 'You are to join the van.'

Torryn felt relieved. He had quickly grown used to his daily summons to join his father swimming at the head of the pod. Leaving Torney and Nayla's high pitch calls behind him, he swam quickly to join his father.

10.
Hunted!

As the days swam into weeks, and the weeks into months, Torkahn watched as Torryn continued to grow in both size and ability. He was proud that Torryn had risen to the challenge and mastered the methods of the hunt. Torryn too swam proud that he had past these most important of tests. He was tired, but he was aware that all eyes were upon him. He knew that he had to give it his all; to face all the challenges that his father placed before him, if he ever hoped to take up his place swimming beside his father, and in the company of other hunting bulls of the pod.

Answering to Torkahn's early morning summons, Torryn swam forward to take up his position swimming next to his imposing father. He could hear heavy breathing coming from Kato, who swam on Torkahn's opposite flank. He listened as his father received news from Kato, who had only recently returned from his patrol swimming far ahead and to the northward of the pod.

Earlier that morning, Torkahn had ordered Rally to swim to replace the recently returned Kato, who Torryn could now see making his way to the rear of the pod and a much welcomed rest.

'I see you, Torryn-Gah,' greeted Torkahn. Arching through the water on a downward dive, Torryn met his father's eye beneath the sea.

'I hear you, Tor.' Torkahn caught Torryn's tone hanging in its tune as his ear picked up his son's attempt to copy the deeper, booming tones of the other more mature bulls who served him.

'You have shown yourself well in the ways of the hunt, Torryn-Gah,' toned Torkahn.

Continuing to swim at his father's side, Torryn held his breath as he waited to hear his next tone. 'You will swim with Kona, today, Torryn. Perhaps he would ask Kola to accompany you,' Torkahn suggested, eyeing an eager looking Kola, who had been swimming patiently a half-length behind. 'Please send your father my respects, Kola, and ask him to swim to join me, called Torkahn. Dipping his head, Kola gave tone in answer to Torkahn's request, before swimming away to seek out the solitary figure of his father. Swimming alone on the outer side of the pod, Kona swam deep in thought. Sensing Kola's arrival at his side, Kona eyed his son closely as he waited for Kola to share tone.

'The Tor offers his respects, father, and requests that you join him.'

'Offers his respects does he?' Returned Kona.
'As he should. Come then, we had better not
keep your noble Tor waiting, had we?

Swimming to the head of the pod, Kona echoed
his greetings to Torkahn as he swam to take up a
position swimming close to Torkahn's side.
'Greetings, Kona. I would have you swim to the
terra this dawning.'
'I am at your command, Tor,' Kona replied, as
he waited for Torkahn to give tone to his orders.
'You will scout close inshore to five hundred
Breath's, Kona,' toned Torkahn. Both Kola and
Torryn will swim to accompany you. You will
guard my son, well, Kona, and see to it that he
does not place himself in any immediate danger.
He is to watch and learn.' On hearing Torkahn's
direction, Kona broke the surface to expel a
breath with a loud huff, before drawing in a
fresh breath and dropping once more beneath
the sea, to swim at Torkahn's side.
'I hear and obey, my Tor,' Kona toned
obediently.
'Look to Kona and hear his tone well, Torryn,'
ordered Torkahn. Swimming on his father's
opposite flank, Torryn eyed his father in a look
of shaded desperation. To have to spend so long
a time swimming under Kona's eye was not a
pleasant feeling. That he would have Kola's
company to help while away the miles of hard

swimming, left Torryn feeling only a little less uneasy. At least he would not be completely lone. 'I hear you, Tor,' he toned. Torkahn heard the tone of uneasiness sounding within Torryn's call. Torkahn knew well that as a future hunting bull of the Tor-Gah, Torryn would have to learn to get along with all those who shared their lives within the pod. It would do Torryn no harm to taste the discipline of Kona as the lead bull on that morning's patrol.

Sounding their tuneful farewells, the three whales parted company with the pod. Setting a strong pace from the outset, Kona chose to remain silent, as Torryn did his best to appear as if the urgent pace was not bothering him. An hour passed in silence, until at last the towering cliffs of the terra came into view. Torryn was feeling the strain of the pace set by Kona. Kola had come to a stop to hang tail down in the sea. They both knew that they could not keep up this sort of pace forever. Raising his head above the waves to get a sense of the world above, Torryn could feel the stiff breeze pulling at his sail, as the sea was whipped into long, racing lines of foaming white caps. The difference between the noisy and disturbed surface of a wind-blown sea, and the peace and quiet of life beneath the waves, was never more obvious to Torryn's wide eyes and sharpened senses. Seeing no sign of Kona, who had disappeared, to be lost in the murk of the sea, Torryn broke the surface to spy-hop in the water, his tail hanging beneath him, as he allowed his eyes to adjust to the light above the sea. Looking toward the steeply shelving beaches of the wind-blown and desolate foreshore, Torryn could see that the beaches were crammed with the fatted bodies of seals of all shapes and sizes.

Appearing as if from nowhere, Kona surfaced very close, his sneaking approach hidden by the shaded murk of the sea. Kola reacted by jumping in the water. To Kona's obvious disappointment, Torryn failed to react at all. Kona was disappointed that his sudden appearance had not shocked Torryn, as it had his own son. Sending Kola a deathly stare, Kona turned his dark eye on Torryn. Torryn returned his empty stare. Submerging with a sharp huff, Kona ordered Torryn and Kola to follow him at a respectful distance.

As the inward tide rose higher, driven by the onshore wind, the jutting outcrops of rocks, that up until now had offered some safety to the sheltering seals, were being slowly overwhelmed by the sheer force of the wind and waves. Feeling the sweeping power of each breaking wave pulling at his body, Torryn looked on, as yet more seals were thrown back headlong into the surf by the tremendous force of the breaking waves. It was the movement of the seals that had caught Kona's eye. Torryn found that he was having to expend a lot of energy swimming against the raw force of the strong swells of the inshore break.

Feeling the heavy drag of the currents pounding against his body as he swam half-blinded through the foaming troughs of the sea, he swam on through a grey murk littered by long strands of weed that had been torn loose from their hold on the slimy rocks. Breaking the surface to snatch his breath's when he could, Torryn could feel the strength of the wind and current continuing to drive them ever closer toward the wind and wave battered shoreline.

The sea was so clouded that Torryn and Kola were each having trouble keeping Kona in sight. Kona's powerful tail drove him quickly as he disappeared, to be lost once more in the gloom of the sea. Unable to keep Kona in visible sight any longer, Torryn and Kola broke the surface together, to get a better look at just what it was that Kona was stalking. Taking a little time to adjust his vision, Torryn focused on Kola, who he could see staring wide-eyed, as together, they caught sight of Kona's awesome figure in the sea.

Kona's grey form could be seen as just a shadow, his mouth open, his teeth bared, his body lost in the tossing whitecaps of the exploding shoreline. Catching sight of Kona as his head appeared from beneath the angry sea, Torryn caught the white flash of Kona's markings that stood out stark against the dull black of the towering rocks. As he watched, the surging waters that broke and whirled round Kona, changed colour to a foaming pink. Looking on in shocked awe, as Kona's jaws crashed down upon seal after seal, Torryn and an equally disbelieving Kola, saw the small bodies that littered the breaking water, as the sea surged, and then retreated under the constant barrage of the ferocious wind and tide.

With waves breaking over his head, Torryn struggled to keep Kona in sight. Swimming through the violent wave action, Kona moved from corpse to corpse, sometimes throwing the small bodies high into the air, before catching them in his gaping jaws, as he again dragged their lifeless bodies beneath the tortured waves. Torryn could not believe what he was seeing. Kona was taking the lives of the seals against the express wishes of the Tor's law. Rally himself had told him that the Tor-Gah did not hunt these creatures. It had always been this way. Until today, thought Torryn grimly. Looking to the shoreline, Torryn could see an angered bull seal throwing his bulk about the beach in a rage of desperation. The wobbling fat of his body moving in time to his unstable waddle, his bared teeth white in a mouth that gaped in a strangled call that was snatched away by the wind. Torryn and Kola lost sight of the menacing Kona as he vanished, lost from sight, in the maddened seas.

Looking to Kola, Torryn felt his stomach turning over. To kill to feed was one thing. To kill for the sheer pleasure of doing so, was something new and disturbing to Torryn. Struggling to focus his vision as the breaking sea washed over his head, Torryn observed the undulating body of the angry seal dashing up and down the spume-littered shoreline. He could hear the bulls barked warning to his many followers who were still in the sea, to seek shelter on the safety of the wind and wave battered beach, so that they might escape Kona's cold and murderous aggression.

In a single shocking second, Torryn's view of the angered seal was replaced by a cloud of flying spray and a wall of green water. Unable to believe his own eyes as he tried not to blink in the breaking sea, Torryn saw a blurred shape appear on the very edge of the wave wracked beach. There was the shaking body of Kona! His entire body free of the angry, grabbing sea. With Kola swimming at his side, Torryn looked on in a stunned silence, as the giant wave receded to leave Kona high and dry on the wind-torn beach. Locked in his jaws was the now stilled body of the bull seal, who only seconds before, Torryn had seen urging others of his kind to safety. Kona's whole body was one blur of motion as his head and his enormous tail moved and thrashed clumsily on the stony, water laden beach.

Feeling himself falling into a deep trough between the breaking waves, Torryn again lost sight of Kona, before he felt himself rising upward on the swell of the crest of the next wave. Feeling himself rising up in the water, he hurriedly scanned the shoreline.

There was Kona! His body angling down the steep beach, the still lifeless form of the once powerful bull seal jammed in his locked jaws. Torryn watched as the next thundering wave arrived on the beach to crash and break in a swirling rent of foaming water, as Kona's quivering body was once more reclaimed by the strength of the sea. Sinking back down in the sea, Torryn again lost sight of Kona.

Enjoying the blood tingling lure of the kill and the heavy scent of blood in the water, Kona battered his way out to sea and away from the surging waters of the shore. Carrying his kill through the strong pull of the breaking waves, he slowed in the sea, taking time to devour the remains of the unlucky seal. With his belly filled,

Kona swam to rejoin a nervously waiting Kola and Torryn.

Appearing through the gloom of the sea, Kona swam to join his young charges. Torryn eyed Kona, his eyes even now still darkened with the deathly shade of his killing madness. Torryn felt his senses react to the strong scent of new death surrounding Kona. Failing to explain his tactics or his behaviour, Kona turned his crazed eye on Torryn as he noticed the younger Tor-Gah watching him.

'I see you, Torryn, son of Torkahn,' toned Kona, his call sounding as deep and as dark as the sea itself. 'Do you stare so to be insulting, whale, or is it that you simply have no stomach for the kill?' Floating frozen in the water, Torryn was unsure whether he should answer Kona or remain silent.

Recognising that Kona was obviously still in the grip of his death fever, Torryn knew instinctively that to tone the wrong thing at this moment could place him in very real danger. It was then that he felt his ear echo to Kola's tone.

'I see you, Kona.' Kona's attention was drawn away from Torryn by his son's untimely interruption.

'I hear you, Kola,' returned Kona, his tone sounding quiet and menacing, sending a cold shiver down Kola's spine.

'Do you dare to challenge my authority on this hunt, my son? An authority given to me by the Tor himself?' growled Kona. Kola had never before seen his father so angry or so wild. Kola bravely held his position in front of his father, his smaller body partially shielding Torryn from the sure wrath of the blood crazed Kona.

'We were instructed never to prey on the seals, and never to kill solely for pleasure, father,' toned Kola, his tone trailing off into a stammering echo. 'To do so is to go against the word of the Tor.' Kona could scarcely believe his senses! His own son quoting the word of the Tor and the ancient laws of the pod.

'So, you have found your true tone at last, Kola?' scowled Kona, his muted call taking on a calm and disturbing ring. Circling both Kola and Torryn in the still breaking seas, Kona swam with a look in his eyes that frightened his only son. Staying close to Torryn, Kola waited for his father's next tones, knowing that Kona had gone too far. How his angered father would react to his having toned in defence of the Tor's law, and what Kona would do, was as unpredictable as the tortured sea in which they now swam.

'You would take the word of the Tor over that of your own father's teachings?' Torryn could do nothing but continue to drift, shocked by this open display of hostility toward his own father by a member of the pod. Kona, his well-muscled tail slapping the deep troughs between each new wave, raged on. 'A bull of the Tor-Gah has the right to hunt wherever and whenever he pleases! All creatures of the sea will bow to the Tor-Gah, and all will fill my belly should I so choose it. If these are your true feelings, Kola, then kindly allow the sea to swallow you from my sight as you return to your precious Tor,' hissed Kona. Kola could not hide his fear of having to leave Torryn to the mercy of his enraged father, but knew that he had no choice. He was bound by the strict laws of the Tor's hunting pack.

Dropping his head beneath the waves Kola echoed his reluctant acceptance of his father's command. 'I hear you, Kona, and I obey.' Kona's dark eye followed his son's movement through the sea, before sending a disturbing tone that carried with it a chill every bit as cold as an Antarctic wind.

'Do not concern yourself with young Torryn, my son. He will remain here, with me, until his education is completed,' sounded Kona, his deathly tone dimming in the shifting currents.

Kola knew then that there was nothing more that he could do to protect Torryn from his father's fearful hold. To fight a bull the size of his father, was for him, out of the question. Although he nearly matched his father in size, Kola knew deep within himself that he could not hope to match the pure ferociousness of the enraged, and fully mature Kona.

Sensing the silent stand-off between father and son, Torryn sent tone to Kola's ear. 'It is best that you obey your father, Kola. To do anything less is to show disrespect. I can well take care of myself.' Studying Torryn through unblinking eyes, Kona could not believe that such tones of courage could come from the mind of one so young. Kona stared at Torryn, not at all sure as to his meaning. Was this young pup showing no fear in his own awesome presence? Or was it a trick to allow him to drop his guard, and to allow Kola to escort Torryn back to the safety of the pod, unmolested?

'Be gone from my sight!' boomed Kona to his son. 'And be sure to hold your tone on your return to the pod.' Kola took this as a warning. Taking one last look at Torryn, Kola caught his eye with his own. Meeting his glance, Torryn sensed Kola's silent message of hope. He watched as Kola, swimming with a heavy tail, slowly disappeared from sight. In his own mind, Kola felt that this could well be the last time that he, or any of the now far distant members of the pod, would ever set eyes on his friend, Torryn alive again!

With Kola gone, Torryn had never felt as alone in the sea as he did at that moment. Sensing Kona's menacing shadow slowly circling him in the sea, he could feel Kona's eyes on him, watching his every move with their deathly black stare.

'I see you Torryn, son of Torkahn,' hissed Kona. 'Now that we have freed ourselves of an audience, your education can continue without interruption. Stay here and do not move from this position,' ordered Kona. In the failing light Torryn watched as Kona circled around him once more, before he, too, disappeared, lost from sight in the surging tide. Torryn could only guess that Kona was again going to play out his deadly game with any creature unfortunate enough to swim across his murderous path.

Steadfastly maintaining his position as Kona had instructed him to do, Torryn swam silently awaiting Kona's return. With the storm now raging overhead, he watched the racing clouds darkening the sky as if nightfall had arrived early. Feeling himself rising and falling in the sea, he floated from low trough, to the high peak of each passing wave; the surface of the broken water littered with clumps of dislodged seaweed and floating plant life, cut loose and alone as he was, adrift in a cold and lonely sea.

With the visibility both beneath and above the sea drastically reduced, Torryn could not see far ahead and certainly there was no sign of Kona returning. To risk using his special sense now to scan the surrounding waters was out of the question, as for him to do so was to disobey the law of the hunt. Surfacing to breathe, he felt stinging force of the driving rain lashing his back. He always enjoyed the rain. The feel of it. he sweet taste that was so very different to that of the salty ocean in which he lived.

Dropping his tail he allowed himself to hang in the water, his head jutting just above sea level. Opening his mouth he enjoyed the feeling of the heavy rain drops bouncing on his tongue. His thoughts turning to his mother, Sorryl, and to the reassuring shape of Nee-Lah, who would even now, be singing her songs and stories to the always fussing Torney and Nayla. Torryn thought, too, of his two elder brothers; of Rally and Daks, and of how he longed to hear their welcoming calls as they each welcomed his return.

Many breaths to the north, Torkahn swam unaware of the potential danger to his son. With his belly full of squid, Torkahn led the pod at a relaxed pace through a choppy sea. With the harsh storm front passing over, he could feel the last warming touch of the sun on his back, as he watched the glowing face of Rah sink slowly into the darkened clouds on the westerly horizon. Torkahn swam well satisfied. While chasing and dining on the squelching and tasty squid, he had found that his thoughts had more than once turned to his youngest son that day.

As the sky began to darken, he had felt the first unease of fatherly concern for his youngest son. Sensing that something wasn't right, he sent tone to Rally who was swimming some lengths behind him.

'I see you, Rally. Is there no sign of Kona?' Rally noted the hidden concern in his father's enquiry. 'There is no tone yet, father. But the day is not yet done, and knowing Kona as I do, I dare say he is riding the young one's hard father.'

Kato, who was swimming in unison with Torkahn, sounded his own call in support of Torkahn's concern. 'If you would consider sending a scout in search of the three, I would gladly volunteer my service for the swim, my Tor.' Hearing Kato's offer, Torkahn turned his eye to the looming form swimming at his side.

Grateful for Kato's suggestion, Torkahn had already considered this option, but had chosen to put it aside. He was aware that for him to launch a search at this time would show his lack of confidence in Kona. More importantly, in the eyes of the other members of the pod, he knew that he must be careful not to be seen to be showing any favoritism to Torryn as his son.

'No,' toned Torkahn. Eyeing the rapidly moving storm front that had quickly blackened the western sky, he made the decision to wait and to place his trust in Kona's leadership.

Having reached his decision, Torkahn gave tone to Kato, 'I thank you for your concern, Kato, but we will give them a little more time.' 'I hear you, Tor,' returned Kato, as again his body curved as he sank beneath the surface of the sea.

Kona had been gone for what seemed to Torryn, to be many hours. Occasionally he thought that he had sensed another killing by Kona, but it was far off, and the sea was far too rough and turbulent to carry the distant underwater sounds to his still inexperienced senses. Continuing to float alone in the sea, he tried to imagine why Kona had left him to swim on his own? A test perhaps? As he allowed his thoughts to drift with the tide, he was startled by the sudden appearance of a number of fast moving fur seals. Their speed was incredible as they darted by, flippers flying, leaving in their wake a trail of tiny bubbles, mixed with their passing scent. For Torryn, it was hard to tell who was more surprised! The seals in their headlong dash, accidentally running into a lone Orca, or the lone Orca, suddenly confronted with the appearance of a panicked mob?

The fleeing seals did not seem to have the time to even notice Torryn, let alone be afraid of him. Something had upset these creatures, and Torryn, who was just starting to build some little confidence within himself, felt that perhaps

Kona was returning to boast of his latest killing spree. As suddenly as the seals had arrived, they were gone, leaving Torryn alone in the sea.

Struggling to gain a clear breath, Torryn found himself being lifted high in the breaking waves, before plummeting back into the deep troughs, the feeling leaving him just a little seasick. He was trying hard to keep his mind alert and off of his empty and grumbling stomach. He was tired and he was hungry. As young and as inexperienced in the ways of the sea as he was, Torryn felt strangely calm and relaxed as he floated waiting for the threatening Kona to make his return.

 The dim light of the end of the day was turning to dusk, a time that Torryn knew to be the most dangerous for all those who made their lives in the sea. And so he continued to wait.

 After several hours floating in near darkness, Torryn was convinced that the blood-crazed Kona was not going to return. He thought of using his unique senses to sweep the waves for any signs of life, but quickly realised that for him to do so, would also risk giving away of his own presence in these torrid seas. Torryn came to a decision. Feeling that he had learned enough from his brief time spent swimming with the van, he felt confident that he could navigate his way back to the pod on his own ability.

Even if by chance he missed the actual area that the pod was now hunting in, he felt sure that at least he would be moving closer to them, should they ever decide to come searching for him, as he was quite sure that his father would, once their patrol was reported late in returning.

To disobey Kona's order to remain was another problem. But he felt certain that under the circumstances his father would give him a fair hearing for his having broken the law of the pod. With his mind made up, and spurred on by a brief but worrying twinge from the scar on his back, he gave several strong pushes with histail and swam into the shaded curtain of the deep. Having travelled just five short breaths his eye caught a distant movement in the murk of the storm tossed sea. As the movement took on a shadowy form, he beheld a sight that chilled his warm Orca blood to the bone!

11.
Zaar!

Emerging from the depths was the sinister and unmistakable form of a large cold-blood. Torryn recognized Zaar immediately. His body was as fat and as round as a bull seal, his flanks scarred by the marks of many an angry encounter. With his mouth closed, Zaar's curled and yellowing teeth were set in a wicked and threatening grimace.

Torryn had little time to react to this new and very real danger. Even if he had been a mature adult, he knew that Zaar would still not think twice about attacking and killing a lone member of the Tor-Gah. Finding an inner strength that he did not know he possessed, he turned tail, sending all of his strength to his tail, as he swam for his very life!

Sensing an easy meal, Zaar's penetrating eye locked onto Torryn's hesitant movements. Torryn was not to his usual appetite, but in these seas a lone and still immature Orca like Torryn, was for Zaar, just too good an opportunity to miss. With his triangular dorsal fin cutting the surface of the choppy sea, Zaar was already moving at speed in pursuit of Torryn. Knowing that he did not possess the strength or the ability to out swim Zaar, Torryn also sensed that Zaar was not swimming alone. Sensing the hidden presence of other Mako, Torryn felt the scar on his back give a sudden twinge of warning. Knowing that a chase could only last so long, and that it would leave him feeling exhausted and vulnerable, Torryn knew that he had neither the size nor strength to defend himself, if, and when, the time finally came.

With no sign of Kona returning, and with little or no chance of help coming, Torryn swam aware that his only chance was to think and act quickly, as his father would have done in his place. Knowing instinctively that to swim out into the open sea would spell his instant death, he made the decision to head inshore, in the vague hope of losing his pursuers in the foaming waves and strong currents of the clouded inshore break.

Swimming hard and pushing himself until he thought he would burst, Torryn swam to the imagined safety of the churning shoreline. But where to go? It was then that he saw his only possible avenue of escape. The long, beckoning tendrils of the thickly, swaying kelp.

Recognising that the kelp may be his only chance of survival, he swam quickly to the surface to replenish his dwindling supply of air, knowing that he was swimming for his very life!

Breaking the surface he expelled his old air, before greedily inhaling a fresh breath in a cloud of cascading spray. No sooner had his head left the surface, Torryn put his nose down and powered on, diving straight down and deep.

This sudden change in direction didn't shake Zaar's deadly pursuit at all. Seeing Torryn swimming only meters ahead of him, Zaar had guessed that Torryn had an urgent and over powering need to breathe. In his haste to taste fresh blood, Zaar had failed to recognize that Torryn, being so young, required less air than that of an adult whale. Luckily for Torryn it took him several crucial seconds less to take that all important next breath, before returning beneath the waves in his frantic dive to find safety and escape from Zaar's jaws. Sensing Zaar was close on his tail, Torryn swam straight down toward the shadowy security of the sea-floor, where the thick roots of the kelp held its waving tendrils secured to the rocks.

Bursting through the towering surf exactly where Torryn had surfaced just seconds before, Zaar's jaws smashed into the sea, his yellowing teeth protruding forward in their search for Torryn's flesh. All he tasted was empty sea as he caught a view of Torryn's stocky tail heading with all speed, down, toward the seabed.

Having foolishly lost the rare opportunity of a good surface kill, Zaar dived swiftly in pursuit of the fleeing Torryn. Zaar did not enjoy being made to look foolish in front of the eyes of his invisible followers. He would make Torryn suffer for that.

With Zaar's presence urging him on, Torryn swam deeper and deeper, until, there, looming before him, was the swaying green curtain of slippery kelp, and perhaps his only hope of survival. Recognising the danger in what he was about to do, Torryn swam aware that he had no other option. Thinking only of saving his own life, he plunged his body through and into the deathly embrace of the slimy, all engulfing weed.

Snapping his powerful jaws, Zaar's triangular teeth gnashed down, catching the very tip of Torryn's disappearing tail fluke. Pulling up short, his blood lust boiling within him, Zaar became angry at his again having missed the chance for so easy a kill. Knowing that Torryn could not remain hidden for long, and that the juvenile Orca would soon have to venture out from his hiding place to return to the surface to breathe, Zaar swam a circular course as he watched and waited for Torryn to reappear.

The strange world behind the solid green wall of swirling weed, was to Torryn, safety at last. He could feel the slimy arms of the kelp rubbing and wrapping around his body. It was then that he discovered that he was not alone in sharing this most dangerous of hiding places. He was amazed to find the wide-eyed and be-whiskered faces of several fur seals staring back at him. It was as if each creature knew of the deadly presence waiting for them to dare to emerge from behind the safety and security of the living, green curtain. The seals appeared to Torryn to be hanging in mid ocean. The thick weed hiding their small furry bodies that hardly dared to move, but for the tiny tell-tale bubbles escaping from the corners of their permanently grinning mouths and pinched off nostrils. For the briefest of moments, Torryn thought that he could hear a series of short, mid frequency echoes - small barks of sound that he could just vaguely understand.

'He's in trouble, this small one!'

'Trouble, yes, trouble he's in. The sea will surely have him.'

'Such a shame. His poor mother.'

'Yes, indeed. Such a shame.'

'Can we not help him?'

'The sea will decide, the sea will decide.'

The rest was lost to Torryn as the voices seemed to move further and further away, to be lost to the sounds of the ocean.

After a time Torryn began to feel sleepy. He knew that this was being caused by the lack of oxygen in his rapidly emptying lungs. He felt his senses begin to drift. Suddenly alert, he felt his body shudder to the impact of a huge disturbance in the water beyond the kelp.

Drifting half conscious and unmoving among the grabbing tendrils of the kelp, his dimming senses reacted to a presence swimming just outside and above the swaying green curtain. Starved of precious oxygen, Torryn could feel his strength slowly ebbing away with the currents of the out-going tide.

His tail felt heavy. He had not realised just how tightly the slimy weed could entangle his flippers and tail. With the very last of his strength, he concentrated all of his senses on the sound of an unfamiliar tone that seemed to echo throughout every part of his body. The tone itself sounding as deep as it was mysterious.

'I see you, Torryn, son of Torkahn, chosen one of the Tor-Gah.'

Drifting in and out of consciousness, Torryn imagined that his exhausted mind must be playing tricks on him. Time was quickly passing. With little or no air left in his lungs for any sort of lengthy swim, again his senses rang to the deeply soothing tone. 'Relax your body, boy, and do not move,' called out the mysterious tone.

'Let yourself fall to the seabed. The weed there is thicker and more easily handled.'

Torryn's first thought was that it must be Kona, returned at last to his right mind, and now swimming to his rescue. But no, this was not Kona's tone. Struggling to identify the possible source of this strange new call, Torryn tried to imagine just who this stranger was who was trying to help him. Feeling his thoughts beginning to drift, he was only sure of one thing, and that was that the deep tone came from one of his own kind. He struggled to think straight. The calming tone sounding in his ear was telling him to exhale. To release the last reserve of his precious oxygen. The deeply musical echo sounding reassuring to his ear. With nothing left to give, Torryn made the decision to place his trust in the unfamiliar tone.

Opening his breathing hole he released almost all of his remaining and precious oxygen. He watched as the escaping air rose in the shape of flashing bubbles, bouncing and bumping on their race to the darkened surface far above him.

How he wished that he was one of bubbles. So light and free to float away on the currents of the sea. Torryn felt himself dropping in the water. In a last clear glimpse he could see that the kelp was much thicker and stronger here. In a last desperate effort to free himself from his clinging prison, he carefully nosed his way through a a clear tunnel in the underwater root system of the kelp. He could hear a faint tone. Distant, yet very close. It was calling to him to follow the reassuring trail of sound that his dulled senses were just managing to cling on to. In a last effort he rolled his body to first one side and then the other, until he found that he had freed the forward part of his body. Finding space enough to move between the thick roots of the kelp, he at last gained some clear waterway. Slowly sliding his body within the kelp, he gave a slight wriggle as he pulled his tail forward with the help of his broad lateral flippers.

'Hear me, Tor-rah-nah,' sounded the same mysterious tone. 'Twist your body as you would when digging out shellfish in the sandy bottom of Shelter Bay.'

Torryn heard this tone and he understood. His ear telling him that there was something familiar about its unique sound. Nearing total exhaustion, Torryn knew deep within himself that this was a presence he could trust. Allowing his mind to travel back to his care free days spent swimming with his mother, Sorryl, and the gentle Nee-Lah, he allowed his mind to flood with the pleasant memories of swimming and hunting in the safety and security of the nursery waters of far off Shelter bay.

Twisting his tiring body in the gripping darkness of the green tinged tunnel of the kelp, he began by gently rolling his body as he slowly edged his way forward through the all engulfing weed. At last he could feel the suffocating grip of the kelp begin to loosen its slimy hold on his tail. He was nearly free.

Turning over, he twisted back the other way, slowly forcing more give from the gripping weed. Feeling the slippery hold of the kelp break free and slip from his tail, and with several short, strong pushes, he felt his head break free of the clinging curtain of weed. Dragging his body from his near deadly prison, Torryn felt the urgent burning of his straining lungs. He felt sick and dizzy. He needed air, and he needed it quickly! With his tail feeling as if it were made of stone, Torryn knew that he no longer had the strength for the long return swim to the surface. He realized then that he may never see his family again. Again he felt his ear echo to the same penetrating call. Appearing like a dream before his eyes, eyes that were so tired that he could barely focus, he found himself looking into the broad, unfamiliar, yet seemingly friendly snout of his saviour. He had a feeling that he was floating quite weightless, like one of his own fragile bubbles. Vaguely aware that he was rising upward, he felt his body break the surface in a whirlpool of water.

Feeling the sudden heavy pressure of several strong pushes on his ribs, he gasped as he drew in his first deep breath in what must have been

nearly fifteen minutes! Taking another breath,
Torryn felt his oxygen starved senses re-awakened by the sound of a tremendous gust of venting coming from the dark form that swam quietly and protectively at his side.

Torryn's first clear thought was that of Zaar. The large Orca swimming at his side seemed to be able to read his very thoughts, as he felt a deep tone enter his ear, to send a refreshing tingle throughout the length of his exhausted body.

'You are safe, young one. The one of which you worry has gone deep, and is in hiding,' toned the echo.

Torryn's first exchange of tone with his unknown rescuer slipped out before he could stop himself. 'He got away?' toned Torryn.

'Yes, he escaped me,' sounded the calming call. 'He would not listen to reason. I had to kill some of those who swam in his wake,' toned the voice. Torryn was glad. 'You cannot reason with a cold-blood,' Torryn toned, his call weakened by his violent encounter. The large bull fired a cascade of spray high into the night sky, startling Torryn as he did so. 'So, my young, Tor-Gah, have you tried to reason with many of the cold-blood?' asked the searching tone.

'I have fought them and I have won. See this scar of combat on my back,' toned Torryn, boasting of his fight with Zaar and his deadly henchmen, in the waters of Shelter Bay. The imposing figure swimming at Torryn's side smiled inwardly on hearing Torryn's response. This was a good sign.

'I do not doubt your tone. But you still have much to learn, boy,' toned the bull. Torryn remained quiet for some time, thankful for his survival, and happy to be swimming in the secure company of another of his kind. The old bull found his thoughts turning to the young whale who swam at his side. He is clever this one. But then he himself knows this to be so. But how clever are you, my new young friend? You have yet to give thought to how it is that I share the tone of the Tor-Gah? Still feeling the full effects of his having been denied air for so long, it had not even occurred to Torryn that his rescuer had addressed him using his own name, in his own tone, and without their ever having been introduced to each other. Studying the broad head of his rescuer, Torryn had no recollection of his ever having set eyes upon this whale before. He was most certainly big! The whale who swam beside him was the size of a small island. Torryn's let his eye follow the line of his rescuer's massive sail, the height of which easily rivalled that of his father, the great Torkahn. His tail was as fat as both Rally and Kato's combined. Following the high line of the bull's back, his eye came to rest on the long, flat tail flukes that he could see were straggled and well worn, showing clearly that he was swimming in the company of a bull Orca of great age.

'How do I address you?' toned Torryn a little nervously.

'When you are invited to do so,' returned the booming tone.

'I am Torryn, son of Torkahn, Tor to the Tor-Gah, and I would like you to tell me your name,' called Torryn.

'Such a large name, for so small a whale!' toned the now amused bull. Torryn tried a new course.

'What of Kona?' he toned, eyeing his mysterious new ally.

'Kona, yes. Was that his name?' toned the bull. 'After he banished your fellow Tor-Gah, and then left you alone, I fear that I could not follow him, for my duty is to you, and to you alone, Tor-rah-nah.'

Torryn had no idea what his rescuer was toning about. He was confused and feeling very tired. Swimming in the knowledge that he had rescued Torryn from near death, and that this whale known as Kona was responsible for placing Torryn in what had been a very dangerous situation, the large bull moved slowly through the sea with Torryn swimming slowly at his side. 'Rest now, young one. There will be time enough for me answer your questions on the new tide.'

Swimming not far off to the northward, Kona swam considering the next move in his deadly game. He had not counted on Kola, his own son, being so difficult. He also hoped that his son would have more sense than to return directly to the pod. Floating deep in thought, Kona knew that Torkahn was bound to question Kola as to why, he, Kona, had sent Kola back so early, and swimming alone. Continuing to hang silently in the sea, his head hung in deep thought, Kona considered how well the first part of his plan had flowed together. Knowing that he was playing a dangerous game, and that Torkahn was nothing if a powerful and worthy adversary, Kona had set in motion a series of events, news of which would soon reach Torkahn's ear.

Using the Tor's youngest son as part of his plot to wrest the leadership of the pod from Torkahn had been his only course.

His scheme to lure Zaar and his followers to the area where he had abandoned Torryn had worked perfectly. The killing of all of those seals had flooded the sea with fresh blood-scent. Picturing a stalking Zaar in his mind, Kona had depended upon the movement in the water, and the scent of newly spilled blood to attract the Mako known as Zaar, and those who swam with him to the waters of the fur seals. Kona had planned and hoped that this would happen.

Certain that the presence of Zaar and his murderous henchmen would spell sudden death for the Tor's youngest son.

Continuing to float, his eyes flashing with menace, Kona considered the next part of his plan. He knew that he must now return to the pod to report the terrible news of Torryn's sudden and untimely death. As the Tor and his female grieved for their loss, he would then make his own challenge for the position of Tor. Well aware that by swimming to this course, that he may have to eventually face Torkahn in single combat.

Flexing his tail, Kona moved with confidence through the darkened sea. He felt strong and refreshed after the pleasure of his recent killings. His shifting thoughts again turned to Torkahn. Weighing up his options. He was near the same weight and size of Torkahn, but he swam well aware that he could not hope to gain a physical advantage over Torkahn in a fight, unless he could find a way to somehow distract him. The death of his youngest son and the grief suffered by his mate may be enough to see the powerful Torkahn lose heart, weakened by the shock of such a loss. It could well be enough to enable Kona to strike a killing blow. Afterwards, he would see to it that Kola took his rightful place at his side, swimming at the head of the pod. Just like the sea itself, he, Kona, would demand all or nothing.

Realising that he may have to fight both Rally and Daks should they try to defend their father, Kona swam confident that the law of the sea would flow in his favour. He calculated that even if he were wounded in his combat with Torkahn, he could still easily kill or maim Torkahn's two spoilt sons' should they be foolish enough to challenge his victory. The leadership of the pod would be his to take by Orca law. The same law Torkahn swam to defend and uphold.

Eyeing his new guardian, Torryn swam with many unanswered questions running through his mind. His greatest concern was that of Kona, and why Kona had behaved as he had toward him. Just as he was thinking these thoughts, he heard his companions tone break the silence between them with a question of his own.
'This whale known as Kona is trusted by your father?
Hearing the question, Torryn did his best to answer.
'The Tor trusts all those who swim with him, until they give him a reason to not trust them,' Torryn answered. 'When my father hears of Kona's actions this day, there will not be a sea big enough for Kona to hide in!'
The elder bull listened to Torryn's tone before

giving tone to his response, 'My life is yours, and your thoughts are mine. I have been swimming and watching you, Torryn, knowing that you may face a threat to your life. A threat your father swam unaware of. I could not leave you alone in these waters without the benefit of my protection, Torryn-Gah.' Torryn eyed the Orca swimming at his side for just a moment, before replying in his most stubborn of tones.

'That my father the Tor chose to place his trust in Kona is his choice to make,'

'That is true, my young friend. And it is right that you should tone in defence of your father's actions. Yet you yourself, have held doubts about this Kona for some time,' the elder whale replied.

Torryn met the elder bull's eye with his own on hearing him give tone to what he knew to be true. 'It is not my place to question the thoughts and actions of my elders,' Torryn replied, wondering how this whale knew that he had never liked or trusted Kona from the first time he had set his eyes upon him. 'I understand, Torryn-Gah,' the old bull toned in answer. 'It is good that you heed your father's teachings. But now I am here to protect your tail in your father's place.' On hearing the older whale's tone, Torryn's call filled the water around them

'I can well look after myself,' toned Torryn. As he sent his tone he arched in the sea, stretching himself to make his smaller frame look bigger and more menacing. The old bull was amused by this young Tor-Gah's serious, yet very sincere tone. As the bull rose again to draw a fresh breath, Torryn noticed that his imposing companion had opened his mouth, momentarily showing the white of his awesome array of teeth. The bull chomped down on a cresting wave, turning it to foam and spray. His tone reaching out to find Torryn's ear in a lilting tone.

'I swim sure that you are well able to care for yourself, boy. But no Tor-Gah should ever have to swim alone.' Considering the wisdom of the elder bull's call, Torryn did as he had been instructed to do by the always watchful and caring, Nee-Lah. Summoning the necessary courage, he addressed his new ally. 'If I am not to swim alone, then surely it is better for me to know with whom I am sharing the sea, so that at least I do not swim with a stranger.' The large Orca met Torryn's eye. 'Are you sure that you should know of me?' questioned the bull.

'To know me could change your life forever.'

'You speak in riddles, old one,' returned Torryn, to his patient, yet very confusing companion.

'But I owe you my life, and I will respect your wish for secrecy as you wish it.' Trying to understand and to show his respect to his new found friend, Torryn rested at the old bull's side as the sea began to calm at the onset of a new dawn.

'We have no secrets between us, boy,' toned the bull. Torryn reacted to the strange echo that sounded in his head. He had not heard this tone with his ear. It was as if the call was sounding deep within his mind. He had never sensed a call that had arrived in his head like this before.

The hypnotic tone sounded as a challenge to his senses. He felt a new and relaxing flood of feeling passing throughout his body like an internal current. Carried with this feeling came a new understanding for Torryn, as the bull's echo continued to weave its unique, harmonic spell.

He listened carefully as the sounds within his head slowly began to form into the bull's silent tone. 'As for my name, Torryn-Gah, that is for you to see, here, within my senses. Clear your senses of everything around you and concentrate upon my call, Torryn-Gah.'

Torryn did as he was asked, but trying anything new on an empty stomach was always difficult for him. 'Time enough for food when you have earned it, boy,' toned the searching call that echoed within Torryn's head. Torryn was startled by this. He had been instructed by Sorryl and Nee-Lah in the ways of the tone, but this was something altogether different. Again he tried to concentrate his mind on the dark form of the bull floating at his side. He found that he could sense things that he had never felt before.

He could feel the water and the way it seemed to move and crackle around his mysterious new protector. He could also feel the others heart beat through the short distance that lay between them. He could hear the sounds of the sea. He could feel the very rhythm of life as it passed through his inner senses. Then he heard a whispered name.

'Sirion!' toned Torryn, slightly awed by what he had felt.

'Yes, Torryn,' returned Sirion. 'I am Sirion. Your thoughts are my thoughts; my life, is your life. You are the chosen one.' Torryn was silent for some minutes as his mind struggled to make any sense of all that had happened to him, and all in so short a space of time. Turning his eye toward Sirion, Torryn quietly put tone to his next question.

'What is a chosen one?'

Stirring in the water, Sirion rose upward until his large head broke the surface in a series of uneven ripples where he took a fresh breath, before once more submerging to place his head closer to Torryn's.

'The chosen one, is one of our kind, Torryn-Gah. An Orca who is born every fiftieth cycle to a father of heart, and to a true mother of the blue,' chimed the now familiar tone.

'Each chosen one is born with a special gift, Torryn. A gift possessed by no other of his kind, but for his mentor.' Torryn found all of this to be quite unbelievable. But the many strange things which had happened to him since his leaving the safety and security of the pod, had certainly began to make him wonder.

'You are my mentor?' Torryn toned. Sirion eyed Torryn with an all knowing stare. 'I am your guide and protector, boy, sent by the currents and spirits of the blue. I am at your service, Torryn-Gah,' returned Sirion, giving a slight downward nod of his noble head.

'Your life, is my life?' toned Torryn.

'My life, is your life,' returned Sirion.

'So you were the chosen one before me?' called Torryn, his tone as musical to Sirion's ear as it was inquisitive. 'I was before you, and there was one before me, and one before that,' returned Sirion. 'It has been this way since the very dawning of our time, Torryn-Gah. Now it is my time to reveal that which is hidden within you, my young Tor.'

The content and meaning of the great Sirion's tone was making Torryn's head swim. Hanging in the sea beside Sirion, Torryn found that he was unable to form a single tone of his own. Sending strength to his tail, Sirion moved forward through the sea, leaving Torryn to follow. He knew well that the information that he had shared with Torryn would change Torryn's young life forever, just as it had changed his own, all those many long cycles before. 'Come, Torryn, let us swim together,' toned Sirion. 'We shall leave these waters and return you to your own.' Torryn arched his back with pleasure at hearing this news. 'My father will surely reward you for your service to his son,' Torryn called. 'We will see what the current of a new tide brings for us, young one,' returned Sirion, as he turned his head to the northward and toward his sure meeting with the Tor of the Tor-Gah.

Swimming in silent company with his newest responsibility, Sirion's thoughts turned to the future, and to the meeting that must surely come between himself and Torryn's father. Having met Torryn, Sirion was confident that Torkahn was a whale who swam a similar course to his own. He would show Torryn's father the respect that his position deserved, but he would swim with a wise caution. A bull as large and as proud as Torkahn, might well have a very different welcome in mind for an ageing bull who approached unannounced and in company of his own son. 'Come, young one, we have far to travel and I have much that I must share with you before we meet with your Tor,' toned Sirion. Hearing Sirion's call, opened his eyes and blinked. Had he been dreaming? Sending strength to his tail he swam to catch up with his new found friend. He was going home.

He pictured his mother, her image floating in the inner sea of his memory. He thought, too, of his brothers', Rally and Daks, and of the annoying Torney and Nayla. Somewhere ahead in the clear, blue sea, Torryn knew that his father was swimming hard, leading his family in the search for any sign of his whereabouts.

12.
The scent of betrayal.

As the first rays of a new day slowly grew into a lightening eastern sky, Torkahn felt the first stab of concern in his belly. Earlier the previous day he had made the decision to turn the pod back toward the wind and sea battered shore, in the hope that it would place them closer to those they were now searching for. As the sun had finally dipped below the horizon, Torkahn had relented, summoning Daks to the van.   'I hear you, father,' returned Daks, who had been preparing himself to leave the pod to replace Kato, who even now could be found swimming far ahead, the forward eyes of the slow moving, and somewhat reduced group.

Moving in tight, erratic circles, Torkahn addressed Daks in a serious tone. The other members of the pod, who had become alarmed at the failure to return of Kona and his hunt, swam to a stop, each venting and floating uneasily in the sloppy sea. Sorryl had known for some time that something was not quite as it should be, after her having spent the better part of the previous day toning her motherly concern to a patiently listening Nee-Lah. Drawing in a deep breath, Torkahn allowed himself to drop below the surface. Turning his body in the water, he pointed his broad nose to the northward. He heard a single, distant tone reach his well-trained ear. He stopped toning to Daks, and with a unique tone, called the pod to an uneasy silence.

'It is Kato,' toned Torkahn, stretching the limits of his senor's to pick up every faint chord of Kato's far flung call. Both Daks and Rally had each clearly heard Kato's urgent call. Swimming far ahead of the pod, Kato had made an interesting and surprising discovery. He had found Kola, lurking alone in the gloom of a darkening sea.

Perhaps now thought Kato, eyeing Kola, the Tor would hear some welcome news. To help shorten the distance between Kato and Kola, Torkahn ordered that Daks swim with him to meet the returning Kato and the lone Kola. With the sun rising and the storm front having blown itself out, Torkahn directed Rally to take command of the pod, before he set out at a brisk pace with Daks swimming at his side. After a strong swim of some sixty breaths, there, in the changing light of the early dawn loomed the shadowy and familiar shapes of Kato and Kola.

'I see you, Kato,' toned Torkahn expectantly. Torkahn looked hard at the forlorn form of Kola, who hung in the darkened sea like a limp piece of weed before him. Torkahn addressed Kato, demanding an immediate answer. Where is Kona? And where in the blue is my son?'

Lowering his head, Kato gave tone to his quiet response. 'I am sorry, Tor, but Kola has not broken tone since I swam across his course.' Turning his attention to a cowering Kola, Torkahn could sense Kola's fear. The younger whale floated uneasily in the sea, his smaller body dwarfed by the much larger forms of Daks and Kato, who swam silently on his either flank. Torkahn swam with the uneasy feeling that something was terribly wrong.

'I see you, Kola. Where is Torryn, my young friend? You must tell me.'
Kola found it impossible to meet Torkahn's eye. The eye of the father of Torryn. Dropping his head even further in the sea, Kola toned very quietly, 'I do not know.' Daks had had enough. The water echoed to his warning call. 'You tone as if you were a dam, Kola! You would do well to remember to address the Tor by his rightful name!' Realising that they were swimming against a strong current in their attempts to get an answer from the obviously terrified Kola, Torkahn called for silence. He, too, was beginning to lose patience with Kola's refusal to share on the whereabouts of Torryn. Knowing that he must bite his tongue, or risk his putting more fear into the already terrified younger whale, Torkahn tried a fresh approach.

Moving forward in the sea, Torkahn sent a near hushed tone to Kola. 'Where did you last see Kona and Torryn?' He asked, taking care to keep his call as calm and as even as possible, so as to help reassure the still silent Kola. With gentle encouragement from Kato, Kola at last broke tone of his sorry tale. Listening to Kola in shocked disbelief, Torkahn could not believe what he was hearing. His silence broken, Kola gave tone of how his father had changed in front of their very eyes into a raging, killing rogue. Of how Kona had slain so many seals that the boiling sea had run red with their blood. Of how he had attempted to defend Torryn when his father had so cruelly and unexpectedly turned on his friend, before banishing him back to the pod for his outburst in daring to tone in Torryn's defence. He had been swimming alone in the stormy sea ever since, too afraid to return to the pod and to face Torkahn's judgement.

Listening to Kola's story, Torkahn realised that Kola must have been swimming alone for many hours, truly afraid of returning to the pod, for fear of not only having to report on his own angered father, but also that he would have had to suffer the indignity and disgrace of returning om the hunt early, and alone. That a father could treat his own son in such a manner, shocked Torkahn. The thought that this same bull should attempt to harm his own son was more than he could stand. That a trusted member of the pod, one of his own bulls, could act to betray him and threaten the life of one so young, was, at least to Torkahn, unheard of. Torkahn stared hard into a frightened Kola's eyes, sensing that Kola was truly afraid of him. Of me, thought Torkahn to himself? No. He is only afraid of his father's tones against me. Had Kona done so much damage to his own blood? And what of Torryn? One thing was certain in Torkahn's mind. He knew that he must act quickly if he was to have any hope of locating Torryn and saving his life.

Looking at the young whale who floated before him, Torkahn knew that Kola was their only hope. 'I thank you, Kola for your honesty. I know that you value Torryn's friendship and I ask you now to guide us to where you last had contact with Torryn. You have done no wrong, Koh-leh-lah, but for your failure to return to the pod as you were directed to do. The crimes of your father will not reflect upon you, Kola, on that you have my truest tone.' Upon hearing Torkahn's call, Kola lifted his head and straightened his sagging frame. Torkahn nosed the young bull forward, and in company with Kato and a still angry Daks, the four dark shapes moved forward at a strong pace through the sea, the dim glow of the new dawn painting their combined wakes a luminous pink.

After a hard swim of some hours,' Torkahn broke the surface and slowed in the sea. The area to which Kola was now leading the small pod was well known to Torkahn. Tasting the heady scent of blood that was still strong in the water, Torkahn sent tone for Kato, Kola and Daks to follow. Together they cruised submerged off the kelp clogged beaches in search of any scent or sign of Torryn. Torkahn's senses twitched to the sharp scent of waste in the sea. He eyed the blurred outline of the many seals lying flat on the rough, round stones of the steeply shelving beaches.

Directing Kato and Daks to make a thorough search of the immediate area, Torkahn took care to keep Kola swimming close by his side. It was not long before Kato emerged from the inshore murk to report a startling, and to Torkahn, a very disturbing find. Following Kato's lead, Torkahn was soon swimming over the stiffened corpses of three large Mako. Their bloated forms already alive with all sorts of sea life, each intent on the slow job of devouring the once great fish, piece by tiny piece. Torkahn felt his senses quiver to the still strong blood scent which hung in the sea. For him, the discovery of three dead sharks proved that perhaps Kola's story was at least partly true. Kato, too, sensed that there had been killing done here; much killing, and only recently. Torkahn could only imagine the terrible fate that may have already befallen his youngest son; swimming alone in these desolate waters so tainted by the strong stench of recent death. Forcing his mind away from such thoughts, Torkahn turned his mind to the three stiffening corpses lying on the sand below him. their presence and sudden deaths could not be so easily explained. Torkahn watched as Kato swam down to more closely examine the pale bodies of each shark. After slowly examining each corpse, Kato swam to report his discoveries to Torkahn.

'Well?' called Torkahn, his short tone sounding his concern for Torryn's safety.

'These fish have been dead for many hours, Tor,' returned Kato.

'How did they die, Kato?'

'Each was killed by one massive blow, Tor,' replied Kato.

'It would have taken a fish of some size to inflict such heavy and shattering blows.'
Torkahn knew that Kato was right. Daks, too, had examined the dead bodies of the Mako.

'Do you think it was Kona, father?' Torkahn remained silent. He swam equally aware that such a killing blow could only have come from another of their kind. But the question was, who? Were these killings the work of the seemingly elusive Kona, as Daks suggested? And if so, then where was Kona now; and where in all the tides was Torryn?

Following the completion of a thorough search of the surrounding beaches and bays, Torkahn at last mustered his bulls for the return swim to rejoin the remainder of the pod. Hoping beyond hope, that Torryn had somehow managed to avoid Kona's anger, and that his youngest son had managed to make good his escape, Torkahn tried to remain positive, especially in front of the others, as he set a demanding pace through the choppy sea.

Pushing strongly through the swell, Torkahn's thoughts returned to Torryn, alone or stranded somewhere in the wide reaches of the open ocean. He felt sure that if his son still lived, that Torryn did indeed possess the necessary and rudimentary skills to enable him to successfully navigate his way back to the pod on his own. Both Daks and Kato had already toned their agreement on Torryn's potential ability to do just that. Fighting back his anger, Torkahn's thoughts turned to the apparently mutinous and untrustworthy Kona. Kona was out there somewhere, hiding in the shadows and the gloom of an unrelenting sea. He would find Kona. Find him and punish him.

Some distance ahead and to the east, the shining blue water was broken by a tall, dark shape moving in company with another. Sirion and Torryn were swimming at a steady pace, their arching bodies slowly rising and falling, before again venting and taking yet another breath of the cool morning air. Torryn marveled at how high Sirion's sail reached into the sky.

During the dark time Sirion had sent tone to Torryn for hours at a time. Sirion, in his slow and patient manner, had shared with Torryn the story of his own life. A life spent swimming in the great inner waterways of the far, far north. A land of snow and ice, and of the highest mountains and great inland seas.

Torryn found that he had, as any young whale in his place would have, many unanswered questions, and they all seemed to be bursting out at once in a flood of excited tones. Sirion eyed Torryn as he continued to give tone to his message. 'We have all the time we need, boy. For you to learn all the ways of the blue will take many tides. And to swim many tides, you must first eat to give you strength!' With Sirion's tone ringing in his ear, Torryn angled sideways in the sea as Sirion's massive bulk suddenly surged forward and down beneath the incredibly clear sea. 'I sense large fish and a growling stomach!' teased Sirion. 'Come, Torryn, we shall give chase to those who would dare to cross our course and allow them to fill our bellies!'

Torryn and Sirion ate well that morning. The sea alive with activity, with the large chasing the small; the quick catching the not so quick, and with the strong always dominating the weak.

With their stomachs filled and with some distance still to swim, Sirion sent tone to an awed Torryn, telling the story of his own life as one of the chosen. Sirion described his own special gifts and abilities that the spirits of the sea had bestowed upon him. Sirion's tone told his story; a story which painted pictures in Torryn's vivid imagination. As Torryn listened to his tall sailed savior, he came to learn of Sirion's past, and of the great bull after whom he had been named. Torryn learned that Sirion had been born and swam under the sign of the hunter. Sirion shared tone of his greatest gift, that being his ability to render himself nearly invisible to every other living creature in the sea. Listening as Sirion gave tone describing these unique adaptions to his Orca senses, Torryn had trouble believing in such a story. A tale that could so easily have come from Nee-Lah's endless selection of legends and tall stories, and songs of the deep. 'You doubt my tone, Torryn-Gah?' called Sirion, meeting Torryn's eye with his own with an accusatory stare. The proof lies waiting to be seen within your own memory, Torryn-Gah.'

Torryn did not understand. But he realized that possessing such a power, should it exist, was surely the most valuable of gifts in a world where sight and sense were valued above all else. 'It was by using this gift that I was able to swim to your aid, unseen, during the near fatal attack on your family by the cold-bloods,' Sirion toned. At last the fog of mystery lifted from Torryn's mind as he realized what had happened on that fateful morning in Shelter Bay. Was this why Kola had been so shy and unprepared to take the full credit for the death of so many of the Mako that morning? Feeling a pang of guilt, Torryn remembered his early attempt to leave the pod on the night he had nearly been eaten by the huge Mako, which luckily for him, had already made its kill.

'It was you, wasn't it?' toned Torryn, as the flood of realization reached into his memory.

'You swam between me and the cold-blood. You saved me.'

'Your life, is my life, Torryn-Gah,' called Sirion.

Torryn now understood that luck had had nothing to do with his surviving two shark attacks in such a very short time. Looking at the large bull swimming at his side, Torryn knew that he owed the elder bull his life. Not once, not twice, but three times! Feeling the scar on his back giving its usual twinge, Torryn swam deep in thought as he listened to Sirion closely, as Sirion gave tone of his other unique abilities.

'As one of the chosen, you have the ability within you that will allow you to understand and to communicate quite clearly with nearly every creature and species who live their lives beneath the sea.' Rising in the water to take in a fresh breath, Torryn dropped back below the surface in a shocked silence.

'You will be instructed in the ways of these gifts, Torryn-Gah. You will need these abilities to aid you as you continue on the endless quest as a chosen guardian of the blue.' On hearing Sirion's tone, Torryn felt a shiver grip his back. An eerie, creeping feeling.

'So I too will soon be able to use these gifts?' he toned.

'In time you will, boy. But not until I am sure that you are ready and deserving of such important instruction,' returned Sirion. Torryn felt as if he was ready to learn of such secrets right then and there! 'Your enthusiasm serves you well, Torryn-Gah,' hummed Sirion.

'But hear my tone, Tor-Gah, and heed it well. To earn these rights, first you must listen and learn.'

'More lessons?' groaned Torryn.

'Yes, Torryn-Gah. The whole of life is a lesson. And all through your life these lessons must be learned well, ready for the day when you, too, will feel the same weight of responsibility as that of your father, the Tor,' returned Sirion. Torryn could only wonder at how any whale could come to know of such things? His head already swimming with all that he had learned from his mysterious and tall sailed rescuer.

Feeling Sirion slow his pace in the sea, Torryn watched as Sirion swam with his head slightly raised. 'You sense, Kona?' toned Torryn. 'No, boy. But follow my lead. Swim close and stay quiet. We have visitors,' toned Sirion.

Breaking the surface together with a whoosh and a welter of spray, Torryn's ears were immediately alive to a strange clicking noise. Visitors? Torryn was unsure as to what or who Sirion was giving warning of. Who in the blue would have the courage to swim so close to two Orca? Swimming close to Sirion's flank, Torryn could hear before he could see those who Sirion had shared tone of their presence.

'Remember to heed my tone, Torryn-Gah, and follow my lead as I direct you,' Sirion toned. 'I hear you, Sirion,' Torryn called back.

'Good. See that you do. Watch, listen and learn.'

The muted grunts and clicks seemed to get louder, as from out of the blue appeared the graceful forms of a large pod of small dolphin. Admiring their agile bodies, Torryn watched the pod moving a school of fish along beneath the surface not far off.

An excited flock of birds, gulls and terns was following, the sky alive with their noise and movement. Swimming just beneath the surface, he swam slowly, watching the birds dive headlong into the seething throng of fish, only to immediately re-surface, often with a fish wriggling in their beaks. As each bird surfaced they would immediately shake their wings dry, before again taking to the sky, only to be seen to dive again and again.

As suddenly as they had arrived, they were gone, the hunt passing on, leaving the ocean empty except for the constant clicking that still danced inside Torryn's head. He thought that he might be dreaming, but for the sparkling silver scales of these fish falling slowly downward. He felt the familiar electric tingle of excitement run the length of his body as he prepared himself to meet with, and to swim with others not of his own kind for the first time!

13.
The eyes of the sea.

Torryn felt his ears and senses being flooded by the persistent tik tik tik tik tik tik tikitiktikitikititikititikiti tik tik tik tik of the many small Hectors' who were each using their sonar to examine his close presence in their sea. Feeling their signals in his head, one popped so loudly that Torryn felt sure that one of these small warm-bloods was swimming right behind him!

This was Torryn's first encounter with the always playful and fast moving "Clickers."
Watching the speeding dolphins' as they sped in all directions, he counted at least forty of their number before he lost track, giving up on even trying to guess the size of their well spread pod. Their small, grey forms seemed to be everywhere at once. The constant clicking and pinging of their odd musical language echoing inside his head. Swimming to keep his position next to Sirion's flank, Torryn remained silent as Sirion glided through the sea while sending an echoing stream of clicks and whines into the seething throng of small dolphins'.

As suddenly as the noise had started, the investigative clicking stopped, to be replaced by the whistling calls of the more conversational tones of the gathering pod of dolphins.

Torryn followed the graceful movements of the very excitable Hectors' as they reacted to Sirion's call. They swam, splitting themselves into two groups, as the first group of five broke off to swim boldly toward himself and Sirion.

Watching in quiet fascination, Torryn observed this graceful group approach to a distance of twenty meters away. They swam close together, each moving simultaneously as their sleek bodies swam through a series of movements that looked to Torryn as if they were acting out some sort of a challenge being made to the quietly watching Sirion. With their tails locked in a 'flaps up' position, the five speeding forms peeled off with the flash of five pale bellies. The slightly larger male swimming in company with the four others, broke off from his escort to swim boldly to confront an awaiting Sirion. Torryn guessed that this group must be the clicker's van. To see these fellow warm bloods so close was almost a taunt to Torryn. He knew that the Tor-Gah never deliberately hunted the clicker, but, even so, these two great tribes of the sea had always managed to avoid each other. At least until today!

The lead bull swam forward to drift in the sea no more than a few meters from Sirion's nose. His escort hanging back, nervous perhaps, but showing no visible signs of fear.

Torryn felt his ear echo to the call of the larger male as he pinged off a series of delicate clicks and tones that were immediately answered by an attentive Sirion. Torryn was amazed when he realised that Sirion could not only understand these creatures, but that he could also communicate with them!

'May I present, Ko-tik, Torryn,' toned Sirion. 'He is the leader, or Bey of this pod. A Tor, like your father.' On hearing his name, Ko-tik turned his short beak toward Torryn to stare down his nose with strong, penetrating eyes that wrinkled softly at the corners. Watching the smaller Torryn closely, Ko-Tik fired a series of clicks and whining shrieks which to Torryn sounded as a confused hubbub of noise. Sirion toned for Torryn's attention.

'Open your senses as you did before, and let yourself feel the sounds, Torryn. Let yourself become as one with the water around you.' Listening to Sirion's deeply hypnotic tone sounding in his mind, Torryn tried. He tried like he had never tried at anything before.

'Hear, Ko-tik,' toned Sirion, 'Hear, Ko-tik.'

Torryn rolled his eyes and stared at the floating form of Ko-Tik. And there it was in his head! He could hear and understand Ko-tik's tone.

His senses jumped as if he had just been stung by the barbed tail of a flat-head! He could understand Ko- tik! Listening intently to Ko-tik's call, Torryn learned that Ko-tik and his pod had been following a northerly heading making for warmer water. The sprawling pod had travelled far and fast under Ko-tik's capable leadership. With the successful birth of many new members of the Yo-ko-ta, Ko-tik swam eager to continue on his course.   Torryn found that he enjoyed the company of these lively, chattering and highly excitable fellow warm-bloods. The constant noise and hectic comings and goings of his fast swimming cousins, reminded him of the lively forms of Torney and Nayla, who though far from his view, swam in the front of his mind as a fond reminder of those who must even now, be searching for him somewhere to the north.

Sensing Torryn's silent drifting, Sirion guessed that Torryn was thinking of his family. To distract Torryn's thoughts, Sirion shared tone explaining to Torryn that he and Ko-tik were very old friends. 'Ko-tik and his kind cover a large area of ocean, Torryn. Ko-tik and his family act as my eyes when I am swimming elsewhere. In return, I provide Ko-tik and his followers with certain services whenever they may have need of me,' toned Sirion. Torryn was sure that this meant that Sirion acted as the pod's guardian in times of trouble.

Ko-Tik was distracted by the arrival of one of his escorts, who chirruped a short series of notes into Ko-tik's ear, before dropping his head in a loyal bow and speeding away, leaving a trail of bubbles behind as he returned to his duty.

Interrupting Sirion, Ko-tik echoed a series of high pitch clicks and whistles. Sirion listened to Ko-tik's rapid delivery of his messenger's highly pitched call. Even to Torryn's untrained ear, the call had the ring and tone of urgency to it.

Sirion, too, seemed to sense that Ko-tik had learned something of the greatest importance.

'Ko-tik swims; sees great Tor-Gah-Toh swim, slow. Following great Tor-Gah-Toh is cold-bloods. Cold-bloods, yes, yes,' clicked an excited Ko-tik. Torryn felt the scar on his back tingle at hearing those familiar tones.

Listening to Ko-tik, Sirion then sent tone to Torryn of what Ko-tik had just shared with him.

'It seems that one of our great cousins of the deep may be in trouble, Torryn.'

But Ko-Tik had not finished delivering his chattering message.

'Saw Tor-Gah; beeg Tor-Gah: he swims alone, alone I see,' buzzed Ko-tik.

'Kona?' toned Sirion, almost to himself, but not so quietly as to escape Torryn's ear. At hearing Kona's name, Torryn turned and eyed his powerful new companion.

'It is up to us to bring Kona before my father, Sirion,' Torryn toned, trying to sound as fierce as possible.

'Perhaps you are right, young one,' returned Sirion. 'But we also have the life of the Tor-Gah-Toh to consider. To let such a fine whale meet such a terrible fate at the jaws of cold-bloods cannot be permitted, Torryn,' toned Sirion solemnly.

'Kona will have to wait to taste your father's justice just a half tide longer, Torryn. But face it he will, that I can promise,' Sirion toned, his call taking on a threatening timbre. Torryn chose to remain quiet. He knew that to have such a friend as Sirion could aid him in bringing Kona before his father. He knew, too, that he must be patient. He could sense that Kona swam free in the shadows of the sea. And Kona had tried to deliberately harm him. He was sure of that now. But the questioned that filled his every waking thought, was why?

Torryn listened as Sirion sent tone to the excited Ko-tik in a series of clicks and pings. Calling his brief farewell, and followed faithfully by his loyal van, Ko-tik swam quickly to join the expectant and eager members of his far flung family. Torryn watched as the clickers moved off, breaking themselves into two separate groups as they swam, with the smaller pod swimming off in a different direction.

'Ko-tik and his van will remain swimming with us, Torryn. Ko-tik has sent some of his pod to shadow Kona, if indeed it is him,' toned Sirion.

'It is him,' toned Torryn, 'I can feel it!'

Ko-tik was now receiving news rapidly from the well spread body of his followers. The forward members of Ko-tik's patrols had already reported that the huge whale that they had reported to Ko-tik, was now being openly challenged by at least twenty cold-bloods! Sirion toned his grateful thanks to Ko-tik's messenger who had delivered this latest piece of news. The agile clicker chirruped in response to Sirion's personal thanks, before disappearing as rapidly as he had arrived, with a flick of his tail.

Moving through the sea matching Sirion's pace, tail stroke for tail stroke, Torryn met Sirion's eye as they dipped beneath the sea, his ear sounding to Sirion's searching call.

'Are you ready to meet the cold-bloods once more, my young friend?' Sirion watched Torryn as he lifted his body to a new height above the water as if he was trying to measure his own immature sail against that of Sirion's own.

'What is the plan of attack?' Torryn called in reply, trying to sound very grown up. Sirion had to admire Torryn's spirit.

'I hope that we shall not have to fight. I am sure that when the cold-bloods set eyes upon us, then they will turn tail and run for the shadows of the deep!' Toned Sirion. 'And if they do not?' piped Torryn, his snout briefly reaching ahead of that of his elder. 'Then they will feel the full power of the blue crushing the very air from their gills!' hissed Sirion, his dark tone leaving little doubt in Torryn's mind, as to the grim fate that awaited any fish who chose to ignore the will of the all-powerful, all seeing, Sirion.

It was not at all strange to Torryn that Sirion felt so little fear when he mentioned chasing off better than twenty hungering cold-bloods. Sirion was, after all, a fully grown Orca; his strength could not be measured, his speed never underestimated. He was a formidable hunter, and an Orca well practiced in defending that which was his.

  Ko-tik had agreed to stand off and observe. It had been agreed also, that Ko-tik would only end in his own bulls should Sirion send tone for assistance. Torryn sensed that Ko-tik and his followers were also unafraid of fighting the cold-bloods. Sirion had already warned him not to underestimate Ko-tik and his bulls.
  'Ko-tik and his pod have a healthy respect for the cold-bloods, boy. But the brave and resourceful clicker never swim away from a fight. We can trust them, Torryn.'

With Ko-tik's scouts swimming far ahead and out of sight, Sirion urged Torryn on to swim at a swifter pace. Ko-tik's scouts had already arrived on the scene as Torryn's ears reacted to the long drawn out call of the huge creature that filled the sea ahead of them.

Sirion had ordered silence as they swam to close the distance on the source of this new language. Torryn could feel the penetrating tone humming through every bone in his body. The deep, base calls of this giant echoed throughout the surrounding sea. The slowly drawn out whines and squeals were soon replaced by a constant and evenly spaced, tok,tok,tok sound. Torryn found himself floating in a pool of sound that seemed to surround his every feeling. To his untrained ear, this call was as magnetic to him as were the chattering calls of Ko-tik's followers.

These new and unique signals reminded Torryn of the sharp tik,tik,tik of the dolphin. This new sound echoed more slowly, and was much deeper in tone. Swimming through a curtain of the flashing Hectors, Torryn stopped swimming, his tail held rigid, as the deep shadow ahead of them slowly changed to that of a whale. And no ordinary whale.

This was the first time Torryn had beheld the sight of one of these giants of the deep. Even Sirion seemed to swim in hushed awe in the company of their distant, but much larger, warm-blooded cousin. Sirion's whispered tone identified the strange rectangular shaped head that showed that their visitor was a mature bull whale. Torryn judged the whale's length to be four times that of Sirion. The rounded body with its powerful flippers and lethal tail must have weighed many hundreds of tonnes. Still unable to send tone, Torryn guessed that their massive visitor must be of a very great age. Hanging in the sea watching the whale, his eyes following every line and bump on the old whale's body, to Torryn, it was like seeing one of Nee-Lah's stories coming to life.

The whale's scarred body and straggled tail told its own tale to Torryn. Of an age old life spent swimming beneath the sea. In his mind Torryn recognized the thick, grey skin that echoed in its lines and channels, the very shape and feel of the sea. The deep grooves and pits in the thick hide, a mark of the many thousands of kilometers that this great creature must have travelled throughout the mighty oceans of the world.

'It is a fine story for such a noble whale, is it not, Torryn-Gah? Sirion's penetrating call entered Torryn's mind like water through a sponge. Startled, Torryn realised that he had been day dreaming, his mind swimming thousands of breaths away. He could not take his eyes from the whale's body. The whale was stocky and immensely powerful, yet the ageing bull was still a sight of great beauty. As he watched, the whale left the surface in a slow dive, driven by just a single wave of his broad tail flukes. Torryn felt his ear echo to Sirion's hushed call.

'Beware, Torryn. Warm-blooded like us this old traveller may be, but that does not mean that he is warm-hearted.' Torryn took Sirion's warning to swim with added care.

As the light increased overhead, they could see the whale's long jaw and his long rows of hardened teeth. Torryn could see how a whale of this size could catch and swallow a Blue shark whole! He shivered as he imagined that the powerful creature appearing before his eyes was more than capable of catching and drowning a young Orca, and swallowing him in a single gulp! Adjusting his sight to the increasing light, he noticed that Ko-tik and his followers had all but disappeared from sight. He felt his eye react to the movement in the sea around the great whale. The sun's rays reaching through the surface to catch the unmistakable movements and profiles of many sharks. Casting a quick look at Sirion, Torryn could see that Sirion had lowered his jaw, revealing his rows of sharp, white teeth. A sure sign that his new friend and protector meant to taste blood.

The ancient whale did not seem to be too concerned that he was being harassed and shadowed by these particular cold-bloods. They had been swimming with him for several days and were beginning to be a bit of a nuisance. Moving quickly through the blue green sea, Sirion and Torryn swam rapidly to close with the darkened shape of the whale. As the light improved, Torryn caught sight of the spiralling Mako. A sight that caused the scar on his back to tingle its familiar warning. There, in the near distance, seen as just a flash, was the unmistakable form of the always hungry Zaar!

14.
Turning the tide!

There was no mistaking Zaar's haunting figure as he swam in and around the swirling body of sharks that surrounded the larger figure of the great whale. Torryn felt his pulse quicken as he viewed their sharp zig-zag movements through the sea. Their shining bodies weaving a deadly net of flashing eyes and sharp, snapping teeth.

He followed Zaar's every movement through the sea. Zaar swam boldly, throwing himself against the bodies of others in his attempt to bully and force his henchmen into launching a final, and probably fatal attack on the old and now tiring whale. Torryn could sense that the circling sharks were unsure about tackling such a foe. Already one of their number lay dead on the sandy bottom far below, a victim of the hidden strength of the old whale's awesome tail.

Sticking close to Sirion's flank, Torryn swam quickly toward the dark water directly beneath the whale. The deep shadow being cast by the whale overhead providing them with the perfect cover to shield their so far, undetected arrival.

Torryn swam in awe as they moved, still unseen, up and under the lined belly of the huge whale.
Sirion swam ready. Their attack when it came, was as sudden as it was furious! Surprised, Zaar and his followers had little time to react to this sudden new threat. Two Mako were already sinking to the sand as Sirion swam headlong into the gaggle of circling sharks. Swimming close to Sirion's flank, Torryn watched as Sirion dealt death blows to two more of Zaar's followers in very quick time.

Feeling the wild blood surging within him, Torryn followed Zaar with his eye, his confidence boosted by the powerful mass of the older bull swimming hard out on his left.
Focusing his attention on Zaar, Torryn continued to follow his every movement through the sea.

Caught completely by surprise, Zaar swam rapidly, his body arching in quick circular turns in his attempt at rallying his henchmen to turn and to make an attack on Sirion. With his heart beating faster than it ever had, Torryn gave chase to four of the smaller sharks who had each thought better of staying to fight a Tor-Gah over the body of a dying whale.

Breaking off his chase, Torryn put all power to his tail as he swam in a broadly sweeping circle that bought him to a position in the sea directly behind Zaar and his henchmen, just as they were closing in on Sirion. In a flash of movement that showed Sirion's true power, Sirion dropped through the sea like a stone, his powerful tail driving his well-muscled body to the deep. Losing sight of Sirion for barely a blink of his eye, too late, Zaar sensed that he was swimming into a trap!

Forcing his nose upward, Zaar swam to alter his course back up and toward the surface. Tiring of the chase and low on energy, many of Zaar's followers had already disappeared.

Zaar swam hard leading the remaining Mako upward toward the flickering light of the surface above. Unused to the stark brightness of swimming directly into the sun's rays, Zaar blinked his eyes, just as a dark shape blotted out the light immediately above him. With barely time to react to this sudden danger, Zaar moved blindly in the sea, his body crashing into one of his henchmen. Sirion swam down from the surface, having moved at an incredible speed through swimming in a giant loop that had brought him back to the surface and above the now surfacing sharks. Breaking the surface, he had taken a much needed breath, before plunging back beneath the waves, his tail driving him downward, and into a head on meeting with his five very surprised pursuers.

This sudden turn about had again caught Zaar completely off his guard. Coming from above where Zaar had least expected an attack, Sirion's solid body glanced between Zaar and the rough skins of two of his followers, inflicting heavy blows on each. Zaar could sense now that he was dealing with no beginner. The larger body of his followers were still well back, all hectically engaged in attempting to deal with the smaller Orca, and the old and by now, very annoyed whale.

In his attempt to turn and to break away from Sirion's oncoming attack, Zaar left his move too late. He felt a sudden and searing blow to his stomach. In the same second his ears echoed to the excited calls announcing the sudden arrival of two more Orca! Sharks were falling to the bottom like so much loose weed! To Zaar's senses the sea seemed alive with the blur of far too many black and white bringers of death! Shocked at the sudden arrival of so many of these monsters, Zaar, swimming in some pain, managed to muster what was left of his pack, fleeing the scene to the south and to the security offered by much deeper water.

Feeling his heart rate beginning to return to normal, Torryn couldn't believe his senses as ears rang to a familiar and most welcomed call! 'Daks,' he called out! Torryn could not quite believe his eyes! But it was Daks! And there, too, was Kato, swimming larger than life at his brother's side. Torryn had never felt such a wonderful feeling! Bursting through the surface in a rush of pure pleasure, he soared high into the air before returning to the sea with a loud slap. Submerging after his short celebration, he swam quickly to Sirion's side. Sirion had observed the arrival of both Kato and Daks. Neither whale had acknowledged his presence as they had sped through the sea in close pursuit of Zaar and the remains of his pack. Sirion swam closer to Torryn in the sea, sharing Torryn's pleasure at hearing the familiar calls of whales' he thought he may never hear again.

Keeping one cautious eye on the new arrivals, Sirion cast his steely gaze across Torryn's flanks. Seeing that Torryn was in no way injured, the pair slowly rose to break the surface together in a cloud of foaming bubbles.

Leaving Kato to pursue Zaar, Daks broke off the chase to immediately swim to Torryn's side. Daks had enjoyed the chase. Daks' tone sounded his genuine surprise and very great relief at finding Torryn alive and well. Circling Sirion, Daks swam unsure as to who this bull was who now swam to shield his own brother so protectively.

'I see you, Daks,' toned Torryn excitedly. 'You have found me!' Daks continued to circle his brother and his large protector. Sensing Daks' cautious concern, Torryn swam to nudge Daks in a playful and welcoming gesture. 'Do not worry, Daks. Sirion is my friend. He is no threat to us,' he toned. Sirion's deep boom interrupted the brotherly reunion.

'Please, Torryn-Gah, tell your brother to stop swimming in circles. He is starting to make my head spin.' Daks did as we asked, but he did not take his eyes off of the large bull who seemed to him to have some control over his youngest brother.

'How did you find me?' piped Torryn excitedly.

'We have been swimming in search of you for many hours, little brother,' Daks toned.

'Father sent us to investigate a disturbance in the sea. We were hoping that it may have been a sign of an easy meal,' called Daks, who just like Torryn, was always thinking of his own stomach.

'We discovered that the disturbance we had sensed was being caused by the leaping and diving of dozens of small clickers.'

'Ko-tik!' toned Torryn.

'Who or what, is a Ko-tik?' returned Daks. Before Torryn could answer, Kato's rumbling call found their ears, warning them of his return. Sensing that he was being carefully watched, Kato swam slowly to meet Torryn nose to nose.

'I see you, Torryn-Gah. It is good to see that you have not become food for the fishes,' Kato joked. His pleasure at seeing Torryn alive and well echoing in his good natured call.

'We have seen the last of those cold-bloods,' toned Kato.

'Their leader has escaped?' Enquired Sirion. Kato did not know if he should respond to this whale who swam so closely at Torryn's side. Kato was immediately suspicious of Sirion, as he heard Sirion give tone in the call of the Tor-Gah. Not bothering to force a reply from Kato, Sirion already knew the answer to his own question. Zaar had disappeared. Swimming alone nursing his injuries, while the rest of the surviving Mako had split off to run in differing directions.

Eyeing Sirion closely Daks called to Torryn, 'we must return to father and tell him that you are safe, Torryn. He still swims in search of you.'

'We search for Kona,' added Kato quietly. Hearing Kona's name, Torryn shifted uneasily in the sea.

Sirion moved forward to meet Kato and Daks eye to eye. 'Torryn will remain here with me. I ask you to return to your Tor and to tell him that Torryn lives and that all is well.' Dwarfing Kato and Daks with his sheer size, Kato looked to Daks, who in turn looked to Torryn. 'I'll be alright, Daks. Swim to father and tell him that I am safe. Tell him that it is important that he swims to meet us.'

'Will you not return with us to tell him yourself, Torryn?' toned Daks in surprise!

'It is important that you return to your father quickly, and that Torryn stays here with me,' sounded Sirion.

Finding a courage that he did not think he possessed, Daks swam to confront the huge Orca who swam so protectively of his brother.

'I do not know your name, whale, or how you come to sound the tone of the Tor-Gah, or what you are doing swimming in company with Torryn. My father will wish to know who you are, and why you have chosen to give orders to those that you have only just met,' toned Daks, as he met Sirion's eye with his own. Sirion closed his eyes and looked as if he was dozing, choosing to ignore Daks.

'Please, you must go quickly, Daks,' toned Torryn. 'I must remain here. It is important that I do. You must trust my tone.' Daks did not like this at all. He had no idea who Sirion was, or what he was up to, but Torkahn had to know that Torryn was safe, and as soon as possible.

'If I leave now, Torryn, what happens if we cannot find you again?' called Daks, his concern for his youngest brother's welfare sounding in his call.

'I shall be waiting right here,' toned Torryn. 'Now go, quickly, and return as soon as you can.' Feeling far from sure that they were doing the right thing, Daks and Kato gave tone to their reluctant farewells, as they rose to break the surface to set a steady pace through the rolling waves. Wishing strength to their tails, Torryn watched as the shapes of Daks and Kato disappeared from sight, lost in the murk of the sea.

Sending fresh energy to his tail, Daks swam greatly relieved that at last he had only the best news to report to his father. They had found Torryn and he was alive! That Torryn had chosen not to return with them, in favour of his remaining with the large and intimidating Sirion, was going to be hard to explain to his father, and to an anxious Sorryl.

Continuing on their swim to report to Torkahn, Daks again sensed a disturbance in the sea ahead of them. Surfacing to draw breath, both Daks and Kato submerged to listen to the sounds of clicking and chirruping being created by the presence of a sprawling pod of small dolphins.
'These clickers have found something,' toned Daks.
'Something has certainly excited them,'
returned Kato. As they swam nearer, their ears rang to the chatter of dozens of the whirling dolphins. A group of the small Hectors' approached Daks and Kato, swimming in their usual challenging posture. Moving through the sea with his eye focused on the fast swimming

members of Ko-tik's pod, Daks kept his eye on the larger male who swam accompanied by four of his followers, their combined calls sounding in a confused hubbub of sounds. Ko-tik had no way of communicating with Daks and Kato without Sirion's help. He was counting on Daks and Kato sensing that for him to be risking swimming so close, that he must be sending them a warning of some kind. Daks sensed that the small Hectors behaviour was in no way threatening.

'Are they trying to tell us something, Daks?' toned Kato.

'You could be right,' returned Daks. 'I have never seen their kind swim so close to us before.'

'They must have good reason to risk their lives in this way,' toned Kato.

Meeting Kato's eye beneath the water Daks sent his reply, 'There is only one way to find out.' Flexing his powerful tail Daks swam in pursuit the now fleeing Ko-tik.

'Bend your tail, Kato. I feel that our presence is required!'

Returning to the exact position in the sea where they had first sensed the disturbance, the Hectors' quickly scattered to the depths and the unseen security of the blue. Through the water ahead, Kato caught sight of the familiar shape of a lone whale. Launching a sensor ping at exactly the same moment, Kato and Daks received the returning images at the same moment! They were amazed to see the retreating shape was now doing its best to rapidly disappear into the overcast gloom of the sea. There was no doubt at all that this presence was an Orca. From their returning sonar pulses, Kato and Daks each identified and sounded their find out loud at the shock of their discovery. 'Kona!'

Kona had not sensed Kato and Daks' hidden approach. The frantic activity and sound created by the crazed clicker's antics, had helped to conceal and to screen their arrival.

Kona turned slightly as he felt the senses of his own kind penetrate his body with a refreshing tingle. He knew that it was too late to run. He was growing bored. After leaving Torryn alone in the blood scented waters of the seal colony, Kona had wandered the sea awaiting just the right moment to re-join a by now, hopefully grieving pod. With Torryn's death a certainty at the jaws of the ever prowling Zaar, Kona swam ready to act.

With Kato and Daks rapidly bearing down upon him, Kona knew that he must think and act quickly. He watched the arrival of the two whales that he had come to know and to hunt with. He could feel no threat from Daks, as he was smaller and easier to handle than the more powerful and larger Kato.

Daks made his approach swimming in a loose circle, choosing to remain silent but keeping a cold and wary eye on the elusive Kona. Kato, too, held his tone, hoping that his silence would force the nervous Kona to break the uneasy quiet between them. Kona chose to remain silent. Before he could share tone with Kona, Daks heard a voice echo inside his inner ear. Or was it actually in his head?

'Torryn's rescue must remain a secret.' Daks shook his head. He had heard a message sent to him through the power of Sirion's mind. He had not only heard Sirion's message, but he had felt it in every part of his body. Daks knew that the message was for him. He was also quite sure who had sent it. Torryn's rescuer and new protector. Daks let his eye wander, searching all round him. If this whale can place thoughts into my head, then surely he knows what I am thinking? Thought Daks to himself.

'Indeed, I do, son of Torkahn.' Daks jumped in the sea. Now he was sure. Daks toned out loud.

'I will do as you ask.' Sensing that Daks was somehow distracted, Kato sent a warning tone to Kona.

'What are you doing swimming this far north, Kona? And why are you swimming alone?'

Kona heard the suspicion sounding in Kato's tone. 'You address me in such a manner, Kato? The last time I looked I still swam ahead of you in years,' returned Kona, asserting his dominance in the pod. Kato remained silent as Daks finally found his tone.

'We should be pleased if you would answer Kato's question, Kona.'

Kona squinted his eye to stare at Daks. 'I have been swimming for what seems like many cycles,' Kona toned tiredly. 'I regret to report that I have sadly lost the company of young Torryn-Gah.' Kato continued to eye Kona with suspicion and without troubling to hide his dislike. 'When you did not return at the Tor's allotted time, the Tor sent out searchers,' toned Kato. 'We found Kola, your son, lurking in the shadows behind the pod.' Kona floated silently in the sea, as if carefully considering his next tone.

'Yes, I ordered Kola back to re-join the pod. As is my right.'

'We have been searching for Torryn for many hours, Kona' toned Kato. Sensing that Kato was about to tell Kona that they had found Torryn alive and well, Daks swam across Kato's nose, interrupting Kato, who caught the warning look in Daks' eye.

'And where is Torryn, Kona? He has gone missing while swimming under your leadership,' called Daks. Catching the look in Daks' eye, Kato remained quietly watching Kona's every move. 'My father swims not fifty breaths distant, Kona. I am sure that he will have many questions for you to answer.' Failing to see Daks sending Kato his silent warning to remain quiet about Torryn's location, Daks was pleased to see that Kona had gained no sense that there had been any change. As far as Kona knew, Torryn was still missing, presumed lost.

Realising that he was placing his trust in the tone of a whale he barely knew, Daks had gained a strong sense of well-being within the whale known as Sirion. It felt right. He could only hope that his father, Torkahn, would approve of his actions.

Kona listened calmly as Daks gave tone to his father's whereabouts. Daks watched Kona closely. If Kona was surprised at hearing this piece of news, then he took great care not to show it. Kola, having been discovered so early, did not help his plan. Kona knew now that he would have to swim to confront Torkahn, only a little sooner than he had planned.

15.
Accusations and Betrayal!

Earlier that day Torkahn had been leading his small search party on the long journey back to meet up with the pod. As he swam, he could only think of how he was going tell his beautiful Sorryl, that he had returned to her without finding any sign of her much beloved Torryn. Torkahn thought of the scar on Torryn's back. The Mako? The image of the now slowly decaying bodies of three dead Mako lying where they had fallen triggered a memory in his mind. He remembered Kola's story of how Kona had taken great delight in slaughtering a good number of seals so close to the shore. The true meaning of Kona's actions that day suddenly became crystal clear in Torkahn's mind. Kona had not been killing for food at all. The sudden meaning of this act hitting Torkahn with the brutal force of a southerly gale!

Had Kona filled the waters around that part of the shoreline with the strong scent of death deliberately? He wondered. Surely no member of the Tor-Gah was capable of such an evil and deliberate act? Torkahn struggled to see beyond the mist that still clouded his thinking.

Kona's murderous behavior might well explain how the menacing group of Mako had come to be in that area at that particular time. Torkahn at last saw the truth. He felt a hollow emptiness in his stomach. Was it fear? No. Torkahn shook himself. His only concern was for Torryn's small life. Following this new current of thought, he knew that Kona, as indeed all the bulls' of the Tor-Gah knew, that this dangerous stretch of weather-beaten coastline was ruled and fiercely patrolled by many of the cold-blooded Mako, and others of their kind. Torkahn felt his blood run cold as he came to realize that Kona must have had every intention of leaving Torryn to his fate at the powerful jaws of blood-crazed killers!

Feeling the strength of his anger building inside him, the grim picture of Kona's daring plot finally became clear in Torkahn's mind. Shifting his eye to Kola who swam in silence at his side, Torkahn considered one last thing. The part that Kola had been forced to play in his father's evil scheme. He now understood why Kona had banished Kola, his own son, back to the pod and to his own certain displeasure. The only other unanswered question which bothered him, was just whom, or what great creature, had slain the three unfortunate Mako?

Torkahn tried to picture Torryn lost and alone in a wide open sea. As a father he understood that Kola's mind must have been torn between not betraying his own father, and his insane plan to kill Torryn, and his being forced to break the close bond of loyalty that Kola felt for both himself as Tor, and of course, for Torryn himself, as Kola's closest friend and companion. As the veil of mist lifted from his mind, Torkahn saw the threat clearly through the murky depths of Kona's treachery. Before he could give tone to the pod to increase the pace, he heard the unmistakable sound of Kato's deep tone at is echoed through the thick silence, warning him of the return of Kato's patrol.

On their return swim to locate Torkahn and the remains of the pod, Kona swam in silence as he matched the pace in his position swimming between Kato and Daks. Sensing that perhaps Daks and Kato might be carrying important news, Torkahn swam ahead of the pod to meet them. As the returning shapes of Kato's patrol appeared through the sea, Torkahn counted the shaded silhouettes of three Orca appearing from the gloom in front of him.

He had been expecting Daks and Kato's arrival, but he had not expected to see them swimming in company with a third whale. To his shocked astonishment, his eyes fell on the unmistakeable form of Kona! Thinking quickly, Torkahn circled To return to the straggling pod where he immediately ordered Kola to swim away.

'Stay close, Kola; but remain unseen,' Torkahn ordered. It is important that you have no contact with your father as long as Torryn is still missing.' Trusting Kola to obey his order for him to remain out of tone and sensor range, Torkahn flexed his tail and swam to confront Kona. It took every bit of his own inner strength to not attack and kill Kona there and then! Breaking the surface Torkahn drew in a deep breath before once more submerging beneath the waves. Before he could form his first tone, Daks' own searching call found his ear. 'I see you, Tor. I would share tone with you father on a matter of great importance,' toned Daks.

Hearing his son's tone, Torkahn sensed the hidden urgency in his son's call. Wishing to confront Kona to demand an immediate explanation for his behavior, and for any news of Torryn, Torkahn ordered Kato to remain with Kona and to not let him out of his sight until he returned. Kona hung limply in the sea, his head bowed, as he tried hard to avoid Torkahn's accusing stare.

Leaving Kona under Kato's capable guard, Torkahn swam with Daks away from Kona's prying senses. When Daks judged that they had moved far enough from Kona, he issued a short tone to Torkahn. 'Torryn lives, father.'

Overjoyed and greatly relieved to hear the news that Torryn was alive, Torkahn floated quietly, his mind deep in thought.

'Where is your brother, Daks?' Torkahn demanded to know. Concerned for Torryn's safety.

'Torryn is quite safe, Tor. He has suffered no injury that I could detect and swims not far distant,' Daks replied.

'Where is he, Daks?' Torkahn toned again as he waited for Daks to reply.

'Torryn does not swim alone, father. He swims in the company of another whale.'

Torkahn swam stunned for the second time that day.

'Torryn swims with a whale that we do not know?' Torkahn sounded in disbelief.

'Yes, father. Torryn is well and swims under protection. He awaits our return,' called Daks.

Torkahn had no reply. He could only hope that what Daks had toned was indeed true. For Torryn's sake.

'It is important that Kona does not learn that Torryn still lives,' toned Torkahn.

'Do not worry, father. I had a message that it may be wise for me to keep the news of Torryn's whereabouts from Kona,' toned Daks in return.

'A message?' returned Torkahn.

'Yes, father. The whale who is swimming with, and offering Torryn his protection, sent tone to me by way of a warning,' Daks answered.

Meeting Daks' eye, Torkahn shared a whispered tone. 'Who is this whale who swims with my son?'

'I know not his name, father. But my every sense tells me that we must place our trust in this whale and his tone,' answered Daks, in an attempt to reassure his father. Torkahn could do nothing but accept Daks' tone. That this as yet unknown whale swimming in company with Torryn had sent such a warning to Daks, was just enough proof that perhaps this whale could be trusted. At least for the present. For the moment, Torkahn swam pleased that Daks had made the right decision.

'You have done well, Daks. It is important that Kona has no knowledge that Torryn still draws breath,' toned Torkahn.

'I have asked Kato to remain silent,' returned Daks.

Torkahn swam to place his head close to his elder son's ear before forming his next warning tone, 'If Kona's intention was to see Torryn die at the jaws of the cold-bloods, Daks, then we must make sure that Kona does not learn that

Torryn is alive. At least until I can uncover the truth of Kona's true intentions.'

Listening to his father put the true threat to his younger brother's life into tone, Daks could hardly believe what he was hearing.

'And Torryn's new friend?' toned Daks.

'We will face that whale as soon as my tail places me before him,' growled Torkahn.

'What of Kola?' toned Daks.

'Kola swims nearby. I must swim to Torryn, Daks. It is important that I hear his side of the story before I can take any action against Kona. Kola will swim with me. Remain here with Kato and see that our friend Kona does not get the opportunity to lose himself in the sea. Guard him well, Daks,' called Torkahn. 'And be on your guard.'

'With our lives, father,' returned Daks.

'Let us hope that it does not come to that,' called Torkahn. 'At least not yet, for all of our sakes.'

Taking leave of Daks, Torkahn swam to locate Kola, finding him swimming as he had directed. Sensing that Kola had detected Kona's presence, Torkahn sent the young whale a short tone.

'Torryn is alive.' Torkahn saw the immediate change come over Kola as his tail straightened and his head lifted to Torkahn's call.

'Come, Kola. We must swim quickly as time and tide flow against us.' Kola swam pleased that Torryn was alive. His only concern now was what would happen to his father? Kona had dared to plot against the Tor. Kola could see no way for his father to remain with the pod after all that had happened. He worried that his being Kona's son, that he, too, would have to share in whatever fate or punishment Torkahn decided upon. Kola hoped that they would not have to fight. He knew that he could not watch such a thing. He had much love and admiration for both Kona, as his father, and for Torkahn, as his Tor. Swimming at Torkahn's side, Kola remained silent, his mind turning to many tides of thought.

Torkahn's eye reacted to just the briefest stab of light that had caught the shining skin of an unknown Orca. As he drew closer he could see that the larger bull was not swimming alone. As the two dark shapes at last emerged into the growing twilight of the end of another day, Torkahn felt his great heart lift!

'I see you, Torryn-Gah!' he called with pleasure! 'I hear you, Tor,' returned Torryn, shooting forward through the sea toward his father in a foam of spray as he surfaced to catch his next breath, before dropping back beneath the greying sea and swimming toward his father.

'Fighting the cold-bloods, again, Torryn-Gah?' toned Torkahn in mock concern.

'They gave us no choice, my Tor,' piped Torryn. 'Is it not our duty to defend the weak and the old? Is it not, father?' Torkahn's response was lost in the piped greetings from Kola. Torryn was very surprised and pleased to see the familiar shape of his friend Kola once more.

Satisfied that Torryn swam without injury, and was no worse for his experience after his having been left to the mercy of the sea by Kona's deliberate actions of treachery, Torkahn shifted his eyes to look into those of the imposing bull, who even now, seemed intent on keeping Torryn apart, and safe from all and anyone.

'You have been dearly missed, my son,' called Torkahn to Torryn. 'It seems that we owe a considerable debt of thanks to your new found friend.'

Looking from his father to the tall sailed Sirion, Torryn could sense the hidden tension between the two great whales.

'I am sorry to have worried everyone so,' Torryn toned.

'You have nothing to be sorry for, Torryn. You are safe and returned to us. That is all that matters. Now, Torryn, please tell us of how you came to meet your escort?' toned Torkahn.

'I am sorry, father. Please allow to me introduce you.' Torryn swam toward Sirion who was floating silently watching Torkahn's every move.

'This is Sirion,' toned Torryn. Torkahn could see that this Orca, although large, was also of a great age. He could detect no sign of a threat through the bull's behavior and how he held himself relaxed in the sea. To not pay some sort of respect to one so old, would not be wise, thought Torkahn, knowing that he owed this whale a debt of gratitude.

'I see you, Sirion. You are welcome among us this day,' Torkahn toned to the silently watching Sirion. Kola, too, gave tone to his own greeting and sign of respect to Sirion, feeling Sirion's eyes upon him. They were dark and glazed, almost as if Sirion was not with them, his thoughts and mind swimming many breaths distant. Kola jumped, as at last Sirion's firm tone boomed out in the sea.

'I would share tone with you, Tor-kah-nah, father of Torryn. Alone.'

Torkahn swam surprised by Sirion's request to share tone with him out of range of both Kola and the ever inquisitive Torryn's ears. That this bull also seemed to have mastered the tone of the Tor-Gah also caught Torkahn's guarded attention. Turning to Kola, Torkahn gave tone to a short command. 'Remain here with Torryn until my return, Kola. Kola could not form tone. Before he could even make a sound, Torkahn and Sirion were already dim outlines, their waving tails disappearing into the darkening gloom of the evening sea. With both Sirion and his father out of tones range, Torryn turned to Kola to bombard his ear with a ceaseless flow of questions about just what had happened since Kona had banished Kola to return to the pod. Enjoying the tone of Torryn's never ending tide of calls, Kola did his best to answer. With Sirion swimming close at his side, it was Torkahn who was the first to break the uneasy silence that swam between them. 'It appears I owe you much for your care of my son, Sirion.' Sirion dropped in the sea and rose again to breathe, before giving tone to his reply.

'Do not thank me so soon, Tor,' Sirion warned. 'My task is far from over, and I fear that yours just now begins.'

'Please explain your meaning?' returned Torkahn to the older whale.

'Soon, very soon now, the Tor-Gah known as Kona will re-join your company,' toned Sirion. His eyes widening, Torkahn toned his immediate demand to the larger Sirion.

'How do you know this?' Torkahn found Sirion's eye in the sea.

'It is not important that you know how, Tor of the Tor-Gah,' toned Sirion. 'When the one known as Kona returns, it would be best if Torryn was not within his sight.'

Torkahn swam surprised that Sirion had guessed of Kona's only very recent return to the pod. Having already made sure that there was no way of Kona discovering that Torryn still lived, Torkahn was interested in Sirion's reasoning behind his only request.

'Why do you ask this, old one?' he toned.

'You already know the answer to that, Tor. It will serve you better for the present to conceal the presence of both Torryn and myself, until Kona has had a chance to share his tone in his own defence,' returned Sirion. 'Time is short.'

Rest assured that what I ask is for the good of Torryn, as well as that of the Tor-Gah,' boomed Sirion.

Eyeing Sirion closely Torkahn did not know quite what to think.

'Time is short, Tor-kahn,' toned Sirion. Meeting Sirion's eye and seeing only truth, Torkahn knew that he must act quickly.

'I would ask of you one last favour in the service of my son,' toned Torkahn.

'If I can be of service, Tor,' returned Sirion.

'I would ask that you swim with Torryn and conceal yourselves until you hear my order to return,' Torkahn requested.

Sirion's eye followed the shape of the slow swimming Torkahn. 'I will gladly do as you as you ask, father of Torryn-Gah. I shall take Torryn and swim with this giant of the deep,' called Sirion. His body will easily shield our presence to any prying sensors. I will await your call, Tor-kahn. Thanking Sirion for his assistance, the two whales then swam to find Torryn swimming patiently with Kola. Torkahn noted that Torryn was floating quietly in the sea, his young mind obviously full of many unanswered questions.

Placing his head close to Torryn's, Torkahn shared a quiet tone with Torryn of his wish for him to remain swimming under Sirion's continued protection. After explaining things to Torryn, Torkahn toned his farewell to his son. 'Take care that you heed Sirion's every tone, Torryn. Do as you are instructed and soon we shall all be reunited, and all of this can be forgotten. Await my signal, Torryn. Sirion will know when the time comes. Then return to my side,' toned Torkahn.

Satisfied that he had done all that he could to prepare, Torkahn looked to the form of the silently floating Kola. Kola was being very quiet and had been since he had heard the distant echo of the news of Kona's return. Torkahn swam aware that Kona's return would be a testing time for young Kola. Pushing these thoughts aside, Torkahn was more than aware that what was to follow was a matter of life and death. What Kona had begun, he would finish. Swimming obediently alongside Torkahn after leaving Torryn and Sirion to swim with the great whale, free now from the lethal attentions of the cold-bloods, Kola did his best to avoid Torkahn's cold, unblinking eye.

Swimming to catch up with the great whale, Torryn and Sirion moved with caution as they made their approach. Not wishing to offend, or to alarm the slowly swimming whale, they took special care to swim clear of the old whale's massive tail. Sirion moved through the sea to place himself directly alongside and within the whale's range of sight. Swimming well clear, Torryn held Sirion's body in his eye, as he watched Sirion's silhouette disappear, to be dwarfed by the sheer size of the whale's colossal body. Adding more thrust to his tail, Sirion moved his body slowly forward until he was swimming staring eye to eye with the ageing and giant traveller of the seas.

Torryn felt himself shiver as his ears rang to a series of low toned calls. He had never before heard such haunting sounds. The deep, base tones travelled through the sea, surrounding him in its unique web of sound. Torryn swam mesmorised.

Just as he had gotten over the surprise at hearing the call of one of the seas largest inhabitants, his ear again tensed to Sirion's next tone. 'Swim to me slowly, Torryn, and do not be afraid.'

As he was about to return Sirion's call, he suddenly realized that he had not heard Sirion's call at all. He had sensed it! Sirion's words echoed inside his head as if Sirion had placed the message in his mind directly from his own. Torryn was shocked to realize that no other living creature in the sea could hear Sirion's delicate tones, because they were made, and could only be received and understood, by the minds of a chosen few. Torryn was not the only one to be taken by surprise by Sirion's secretive tones.

The great whale's eye widened in surprise as it came to realise that these smaller whales, who had so bravely driven off the pestering Mako's prolonged attack against him, apparently meant no further harm, and were in their clumsy way, trying to share tone with him. Sirion swam as close as he dared to the much larger whale. After swimming for several minutes in complete silence, he toned his first greetings to the great one.

'I see you, old one...,' There was no answer, just the ever present sound of the sea and the smaller waves breaking against the huge flanks of this true traveller of the sea.

Again Sirion gave tone to his halting greeting. Before he could finish, Torryn heard for the second time the ageless tone of the whale.

'I heeear youuuuu...coussssin,' toned the deeply melodic voice. 'I trussst that I have not passsst from the ssstorm and into the eye of the hurricane?'

To an astonished Torryn, the whale's ancient tones sounded like the call of the sea itself.

He listened as Sirion toned his response to the whale in a slow and respectful manner.

'I hear you, great one. Please rest assured that we mean you no harm.'

The whale's oval eye seemed to seek out Torryn in the sea, as the deep voice again spoke in the ancient language of his kind. 'You have my voice, whale?'

'I know of your language, great one,' toned Sirion.

'Then I will shhhhhare tone with yooouuuu, whale, as it amussses me to doooo ssooo, and yoouuuu shhhhall be rewarded through heeeearing my tone,' called the whale. 'And I will have shhhooown that I am not sssooo great asss to not recognise something that is new to me. I am known as Ko-luk-tou,' toned the whining bass of the whale. 'I would thank you both for your ssservice to me, but I was in no real danger. The shhhaarp teeth would soon have grown booored with meeee.'

Sirion knew better than to argue with one who had attained such great age. 'As you wish, great one,' he toned, lowering his head in a very dignified bow. 'I swim as Sirion, guardian to Torryn, son to the Tor of the Tor-Gah.'

'Indeed...,' toned a seemingly unimpressed Ko-luk-tou. 'I must be honoured then, to be sssswimming in the presence of such greatnessss,' toned the old whale.

As he was about to send his own greetings to the great whale, Torryn caught the look in Sirion's eye. Sirion had chosen not to hear the mocking tones of the old whale. Torryn listened as Sirion toned his further respects and asked if there was anything further that the Tor-Gah could do, for this ageing, and seemingly very ungrateful whale. The old whale sang his reply in the ancient manner of his kind, with Sirion and Torryn each feeling slightly hypnotised by the eerie sounds of his timeless call.

'I have ssswum these ssseas for more than eighty cccycles,' toned Ko-luk-tou. 'I have travelled faaarrrr and ssseen all in my long time in the blue. I must travel on. On to my last great dive in the distant waters, where the cold is king...and the sea is deep and inviting.' Although the whale's story was fascinating to listen to, Torryn could not stop the flow of his thoughts following in his father's wake.

Swimming alert but relaxed, Torkahn moved slowly through the water with Kola swimming at his side, he could feel the chill of the early morning sea sweeping over his body. He was tired. Tired of waiting. Tired of not knowing why Kona should have acted as he had to shatter the silent trust that bound them all so closely together. He swam in silence trying to understand the currents that had guided him to this point in time. He knew that his leadership depended on one thing. Trust. 'Trust, Tor?' toned Kola. Torkahn realised that he toned aloud. He eyed Kola swimming in the sea beside him.

'Yes, Kola. We must have trust. You must learn to trust me, and know that what I do is always for the good of all who would follow me,' toned Torkahn. Kola remained quiet. Not sure if he should send tone to his Tor at such a time.

'Do you feel that a Tor should be able to trust in the thoughts and deeds of all those who swim with him, Kola?' called Torkahn. Hearing Torkahn's tone, Kola swam unsure if he should answer such a question. 'Yes, Tor,' toned Kola after some seconds.

'And in return they must trust and have confidence in him and his leadership,' returned Torkahn. 'Without trust, Tor, there is nothing,' agreed Kola.

'I am glad that you, of all my followers, understand this, Kola,' toned Torkahn. It was then that Kola realised that Torkahn had really been toning of his father, and of how Kona had broken that very same trust through his ruthless actions.

As the sun began its climb into the dawn sky, Torkahn swam toward his confrontation with the scheming Kona. Sensing that they were nearing Daks and Kato's last position, he turned his thoughts to Kola, who swam quietly and obediently at his side. Not wishing to alarm Kola, he ordered Kola away. 'Leave me now, Kola. Swim for twenty breaths to the east and await my call for you to return. Go now, quickly, Kola,' called Torkahn.
'Try not to worry, Kola. I ask you to leave me for your own sake, and for that of Torryn.'
Kola dipped his head. He understood that Torkahn was trying to spare him from witnessing what was about to come. Watching Kola's tail disappear into the gloom of the early morning sea, Torkahn watched until Kola's shadow was no longer visible in the sea. Swimming in silent thought, he surfaced to take a breath. Now he must deal with Kona. Dipping back beneath the sea, he swam to confront Kola's father.

Through the dim light of the dawn Torkahn's eye soon focused on the images of the three darkened forms emerging through the sea ahead of him.

Both Daks and Kato, who had spent the preceding hours guarding the silently brooding Kona, noticed the absence of any kind of formal greeting made to Kona by their Tor on his return. Torkahn tensed in the sea at his first glimpse of Kona's awkward form, as he appeared through the gloom swimming between and slightly ahead of his two unofficial escorts. As the three darkened forms came to a slow cruising speed, Torkahn gave tone to Kona.
 'Face me, whale!' boomed Torkahn.
Kona, his head slightly bowed, his hooded eyes looking elsewhere, chose to remain silent.
 'You have been gone a good many hours, Kona. And now I must ask you, where is my son, Torryn?'
Kona was slow to respond. He had felt rather than seen Kola's presence somewhere nearby. And now he must face Torkahn. Breaking the surface, he drew in a deep breath before giving tone. 'I am deeply sorry, Tor, but I have been unable to find Torryn following our forced separation while on the hunt. I have been swimming many hours in search of the young one, Tor, but I fear he is lost to us.'

'I cannot believe what I am hearing!' boomed Torkahn. 'You, Kona, were ordered to escort Torryn. To allow yourself to become separated from your charge is unacceptable, Koh-neh-nah!' Torkahn eyed Kona closely as Kona dropped his head, his slender tone continuing to push his tide of lies and half truths. 'The seas were huge, my Tor,' Kona continued, his own tone sounding as an unsteady hiss; 'the waters were churned into a cloudy....' 'Enough of your excuses, Kona, stay your tone!' ordered Torkahn, the increased volume of his threatening call sounding his mounting anger. The strength of Torkhan's call sounding as a final warning to Kona.

'I have heard from Kola, your own son, of your behaviour in the waters of the seal and their kind.' Kona held his tone. Torkahn watched Kona's slitted eyes darting from shadow to shadow. Kona carefully formed his next tone to Torkahn. 'I was instructing Torryn and Kola in the art of Terra-hunting, Tor,' as he described his his own sudden, and brutal attack on the bull seal on the stones of the beach itself. It seemed to Torkahn that Kona was almost enjoying defending his own murderous actions.

Torkahn had heard more than enough.

'SILENCE, Koh-neh-nah! You, in your own son's tone, stand accused of the slaughter of many of the innocent and their kind,' sounded Torkahn, his tone building in strength, until the terrifying sound seemed to force Kona downward in the sea. Torkahn's jaw hung open, his rows of teeth gleaming in the dull light. Sensing that Torkahn had far from finished with the disgraced Kona, Daks and Kato backed in the sea, moving away from the two larger bulls, as Torkahn and Kona continued to hang in the water, facing each other, broad nose to broad nose.

'I accuse you, Kona, of placing Torryn in danger by your deliberate action of flooding those waters with the freshly spilled blood of your defencless victims,' accused Torkahn.

'You knew full well that those waters are well-used by the cold-bloods, Kona. Yet still you set about inviting their attention by this deliberate act of wanton killing.' Kona was unsure how to proceed. Torkahn had obviously found no trace of the missing Torryn. Perhaps he was even now filling Zaar's stomach? Kona did hope so. Strengthened by this thought, Kona swam to confront Torkahn, his tone sounding in his own defence.

'I have done nothing I should be ashamed of, Tor,' boomed Kona. 'Kola chose to disobey my direct command and paid the price, as any young whale should.'

'Yes, Kola paid a price, Kona,' returned Torkahn. 'He paid it by feeling that he could not return to his rightful place in the pod after defending my tone of law, in protection of the lives that you yourself, admit that you have taken against my tone.' Torkahn paused before continuing, his eye never leaving Kona's head.

'Kola has shared tone with me of your attack on Torryn, before your most unfortunate separation,' his deadly call sounding as barely a whisper in the sea. Kona lowered his head before loosing off a blast of old breath high into the darkening sky in a show of defiance.

Distant thunder echoed across the sea, as yet another dark cloud front threatened from the south. 'I made no such attack on Torryn!' sounded Kona. 'Like Kola, the young one had much to learn if he wished to survive in my world!'

'You tone as if my son were already dead, Kona! Perhaps you know more than you are willing to tone after all?' hissed Torkahn, as he pushed his enormous body forward to place his eye only inches away from Kona's. Torkahn hung in the sea, his eyes dark, his forced silence sending an eerie chill down Kona's spine.

Kona could feel the looming presence of both Kato and Daks keeping station in the rolling water beside and to his rear, using small flicks of their powerful tails.

'I know nothing of Torryn, or of any fate that may have befallen him,' toned Kona.

'Only Torryn himself could tell you of Kola's behaviour that morning, and of my own concern for Torryn's proper education.' Torkahn fixed Kona with a look that forced Kona to meet his eye. Kona struggled not to blink as he felt the burning energy behind Torkahn's dull stare.

Tempted as he was to finish Kona's miserable life then and there, Torkahn forced himself to look away from Kona, whose rigid form swam before him. Rising to the surface to vent and to breathe, Torkahn swam ready to summon Torryn. Allowing himself to sink slowly back beneath the sea, Torkahn returned to swim nose to nose with the solitary Kona. Kona could feel Kato and Daks slowly closing in on him, with Torkahn floating directly in front of him, the look in his dark eyes daring Kona to break and run. Torkahn came to a halt in the sea. When it came, Torkahn's tone sounded cold and accusing.

'Kona, as one of my bulls you deserve a fair hearing in the matter of your supposed failure to watch over both Kola and Torryn, while ranging on a patrol under my orders. You have toned your side of this story, Kona, as has your own son, Kola. We shall now hear the truth,' toned Torkahn. Torkahn rose in the sea to break the surface. Raising his tail, he slapped the surface of the sea with his flukes.

This was the pre-arranged signal he had agreed on with Sirion. Kona started in the sea, unsure as to what had made Torkahn act in this manner. Sensing Torkahn's signal as it vibrated through the sea, Sirion and Torryn, after making their apologies to the old whale, left Ko-Luk-Tou's company to swim to meet Torkahn, and to face Kona's bluff.

Feeling his senses ringing to the incoming presence of other Orca, Kona blinked. He could not believe the sight that appeared swimming through the gloom of the sea. Appearing before him like a ghost out of the blue, was the unmistakable form of Torryn.
  Torkahn kept his eye fixed firmly to Kona's head. 'I see you, Torryn-Gah,' greeted Torkahn. Kona watched as Torryn moved through the sea to greet his father and to swim close by his side. 'I see you, Kona,' toned Torryn respectfully. Kona shook his head, thinking that his senses must be playing tricks on him. Surely this could not be Torryn appearing as if by magic through the gloom? He could not believe his senses! How was it possible that the young Tor-Gah had managed to swim free of Zaar's jaws?

Torkahn watched with interest the hint of surprise appear in Kona's eyes. Just a hint, no ore: but more than enough for Torkahn.

'Now we will discover the truth of things, Kona?' toned Torkahn. Hugging Torkahn's flank, Torryn was enjoying swimming close to his father. After sharing tone with Kola, and sharing his thoughts with the wise Sirion, Torryn had come to realise just how close he had come to being Kona's unsuspecting victim. What he could not understand, was why? Torryn eyed Kona carefully. He felt strange. He felt no fear as he approached Kona. Kona floated in silence, staring wide-eyed at Torryn as if he should not be there. With solemn encouragement from Torkahn, Torryn began to quietly give tone. He gave tone of how he had been left alone in a heavy sea, with the harsh words of Kona still ringing in his ears. He toned, too, of how he had first set eyes on the deathly shape of Zaar, and of how he had been chased by the killer into the slimy, green curtain of the swirling kelp.

Finishing his story, Torryn went on to describe how three of Zaar's followers had come to meet their most violent and sudden end at the eye of some unknown, but very powerful presence.

Disturbed by Torryn's unexpected appearance, Kona remained silent as Torryn finished giving tone to his side of the story. Torryn floated quietly staring at Kona. Moving toward Torkahn in the sea, Kona attempted to navigate his way through Torryn's well toned tale. 'Surely Tor, you must understand that the boy is young and well able to exaggerate certain things, that, at the time, must have seemed very strange to him.' Kona's call sounded smooth and surprisingly calm to Torkahn's ear. Torkahn flung himself forward in the sea, the sudden movement taking Kona by surprise!

'The only thing I find strange here, Koh-neh-nah, is your miserable inability to be able to give tone to the truth!' boomed Torkahn. Startled by Torkahn's sudden movement and outburst, Kona attempted to steer the situation in his own favour in his position as a hunting bull in the Tor-Gah. 'I have done everything in my power to both serve and protect, Torryn!' Barked Kona in a final act of blatant defiance.

The building seas became rough as the whitecaps broke in waves over the small assembly of Orca. Beneath the sea the sounds of the racing wind and breaking seas lost their power as the groups ears echoed to an accusing tone.

'You have failed miserably to do either, Kona!' toned a deep call that was as yet, unknown to Kona. This strange new tone seemed to be coming from behind him, yet Kona could not sense any defensive movement from either Kato or Daks, at the arrival of this new and ominous presence.
Turning in the sea Kona found himself looking into the broad, round face of a truly large Orca.

'It is good to meet your eye at last. I grew so tired of always viewing your tail as you swam so quickly from your duty' toned Sirion, with a rumbling menace. His accusation sounding in the sea for all to hear. Kona stilled himself in the water at the appearance of the large and threatening Sirion.

'Who are you?' demanded Kona, eyeing this new threat. Kona turned to Torkahn, and, as he did so, Kona broke the choppy surface, vented hard and then dropped back beneath the waves before toning... 'Who is this... outsider? He has no right to be heard here!'

'He has earned every right to echo his thoughts,' toned Torkahn.

'What could an outsider have to say that could be of any importance,' returned a very nervous sounding Kona, as he swam to round on Sirion.

'If you would cease your empty toning, and with your Tor's permission, I will explain all, Koh-neh-nah...,' boomed Sirion, his teeth showing plainly in his half open jaws.

With Torryn now swimming close to Sirion's grey bulk, Kona felt the first threads of real fear grip his now empty stomach.

With a nod from Torkahn, Sirion gave tone to those around him, 'Members of the Tor-Gah, here me now. I have been following the Tor-Gah for many moons. Until this day, I have watched and listened in silence since the birth of the one

named Tor-rah-nah. Since that day, I have never let the whale known as Torryn wander far from my all-seeing eye. His life, is my life,' toned Sirion, 'for he is the chosen one.'
Kona could only float and wonder as he eyed Sirion and Torryn, who swam at Sirion's side.

'What nonsense talk is this,' barked Kona. 'You would listen to the ravings of an old has-been? A whale who admits that he has been silently stalking the pod, unseen, for many days?'

'You would do well to be silent and to listen, Kona,' toned Torkahn.

Kona held his tone. His mind racing to assess this new and disturbing turn of events. Sirion continued as Kona seemed to wither in front of the on looking bulls. Sirion gave tone of how he had first observed Kona on his arrival to assist his son, Kola, in the guarding of the females and their young in the far off safety of Shelter Bay.

Torryn went on to tone of how Kona had seen Zaar and his henchmen as they were forming their attack, and had how Kona had deliberately held back his attack in support of Kola and the females, placing them all in very real danger. Torryn watched as Kona sank visibly in the sea, his ears echoing to Sirion's accusing call as Sirion gave tone of how Kola had gallantly attacked the cold-bloods with the ready assistance of Torryn.

'You, Kona, deliberately aided the cold-bloods in their attack,' accused Sirion, his tone entering the bodies of every whale present.

'You did not attack these fish, Kona, as you should have. Instead, you lay well back to allow the sharp teeth to mount their attack on the unsuspecting females and their young. It was I, Kona, who acted on your behalf that day,' toned Sirion.

The chilling echo of Sirion's deathly tone hanging about Kona like a weight of stones.

'I did not sense your presence,' toned Kona defensively, his call sounding unsure.

'Because I did not permit you to do so,' returned Sirion, his deep tone giving life to the truth. 'Only the whale known as Rally has ever come close to detecting my hidden presence,' toned Sirion, to a much surprised Torkahn.

'I will have to watch that one, too, I think,' called Sirion.

Kona continued to float in silence, surrounded by the members of his pod that he had never really taken the trouble to come to know. Torkahn stared at Kona's sagging form, his guilt showing clearly for all to witness. It both angered and saddened Torkahn that one of his own bulls had acted to betray him in such a savage way. But the truth of Torryn's tone, together with Sirion's eyewitness account of Kona's treachery, had shown Torkahn the depth of Kona's treacherous scheming, that could so easily have resulted in Torryn's death.

Buoyed by the safe return of his son, Torkahn turned in the sea to face Kona, his deep call sounding for all to hear.

'Koh-neh-nah.' Kona flinched at the impact of Torkahn's harsh tone.

'Your actions this day show me that you have no respect for either myself as your Tor, nor toward the pod Tor-Gah. Instead of standing to challenge me openly as you should have done, you chose to plan and to scheme against me in secret. You planned to not only kill the blood of my blood, Kona, but you also surely desired my position as Tor!'

Kato and Daks continued to watch, listen and to float in silence, the words of the Tor bringing new meaning to their duty as Kona's escort.

'I would circle and fight you here and now, Koh-neh-nah, if that is what you truly desire,' toned Torkahn, his tone sounding in a deathly call. 'But hear me well, Koh-neh-nah, for you will surely die!'

16.

Let the punishment fit the crime.

Tensing in anticipation, Kato and Daks waited for Kona to make the next move in this very dangerous game. Torkahn held still in the sea, his eye never straying from Kona's own dull stare. 'Why, Kona? Why did you swim to act against me?'

Kona considered Torkahn's tone. With the arrival of Sirion, Kona realised that his chances for success had all but drained away with the out-going tide.

'Why, Torkahn? You ask why?' toned Kona. 'Because I had grown tired of swimming to the soft tone of another that is why! I cannot swim in the wake of a whale who chooses to swim away from our true course. I have a right to taste the blood of those that I choose to fill my belly!'

Torkahn could see the defiance burning in Kona's eyes. Kona continued, his tone sounding more like a hiss. 'You give your weed-brained sons' responsibilities that they are not up to carrying,' Kona toned accusingly. You spoil them, Tor-kah-nah. You arrange mates for Rally and Daks, and then you promise the next dam to Kato? You do these things with no thought to my position in your van. I have served you well. I have helped to fill the greedy bellies of your family, and this is how you choose to repay my service?' Kona's strangled call grew louder as he continued to rant at how he thought Torkahn had acted deliberately against him. Torkahn could see that Kona had let such imagined slights burrow like worms into his brain.

'Don't look at me with your pity, Tor. I am what I am,' hissed Kona. 'My failure is yours to share, Tor-kahn!'

For Torkahn, there was really little more that he could tone. 'It is true, Kona, that you have been swimming in my wake. But you do so at my order and with my permission,' toned Torkahn.

'Your life is mine, Kona. You swim to my tone as Tor. Unless you feel that you would like to challenge my leadership, as any bull with honour would have done in your place?' challenged Torkahn.

Watching Kona's wild eyes Torkahn could sense that Kona's guilt was as obvious as his madness. He was growing impatient at hearing Kona's excuses and accusations. Just as he was about to address Kona for the final time, he felt, rather than hearing, a calming tone sounding deep within his head. Keeping one eye fixed firmly on

Kona, Torkahn carefully scanned the waters around him. He could find no sign of either Torryn or Sirion, who must have slipped away earlier. He was glad that both Torryn and Kola had been spared Kona's theatrics. He also had no doubt that the tone he was hearing belonged to the mysterious Sirion.

'I see you, Torkahn, and I would share tone with you now,' sounded the voice in Torkahn's head. Torkahn seemed to know instinctively just where the looming shadow of Sirion could be found. Kona could sense that Torkahn was distracted. Giving tone to Kato and Daks to guard Kona with their lives, Torkahn swam to answer Sirion's secretive call. Kato and Daks stared at each other in a gentle confusion; neither of them willing to break the Tor's standing order for total silence as they watched Torkahn disappear into the night-time gloom.
Watching Torkahn swim off into the murk of the darkening sea, Kona sensed that perhaps Torkahn was weakening. Perhaps there may still be a slim chance. Had Torkahn lost his nerve?

As he knew he would, Torkahn found Torryn and Sirion swimming in company with the elderly whale known as Ko-luk-tou. The ancient whale, now well rested after the hectic attack of Zaar and his gang, swam peacefully in a giant circle around the now distant Kona and his alert guard.

Torkahn could see Torryn, his shape moving through the sea, swimming close in and alongside the old whale. Torkahn felt his ear tingle to Sirion's muted tone as the older Orca appeared as if by magic, swimming at his side.

'I trust that you might forgive my untimely interruption, Tor, but I thought it important that we meet,' toned Sirion. 'I know that I have no right to share tone with you of such matters, Tor. It is your pod; your responsibility, and I am, after all, as Kona described me, an outsider.' Torkahn eyed the older bull swimming at his side.

'You have more than earned your right to share your concerns with me, Sirion. It was you who returned my son to me, and for that my debt to you is as deep as the deepest ocean,' toned Torkahn gratefully. On hearing Torkahn's reply, Sirion paid respect to Torkahn with a bow of his head. 'It is about Kona that I wish to share tone, Tor.' Sirion saw Torkahn's tail stiffen at his call.

'I owe you a personal debt of honour, Sirion,' returned Torkahn, 'but please, do not involve yourself in something that must be left to me, and to me alone.'

'I hear you, Tor......but I must share tone on behalf of Torryn. To give voice to his future,' toned Sirion. Sensing that the wise old Sirion was using his son to leverage his own interests, Torkahn made his reply.

'Very well, Sirion, I will hear your tone.'

'To challenge Kona is your hard won right, Tor. That is as it should be. But I must warn you, that this course will only lead to Kona's death. This price must be paid, as surely as the mighty Rah rises each new dawn. For the Tor to allow Kona to live would be to show weakness in front of his bulls,' toned Sirion.

'I am aware of this,' toned Torkahn, impatient to return to Kona, and to finish what he had begun. He waited as Sirion continued.

'Should you indeed vanquish Kona, then what of Kola, son of Kona and good friend to Torryn-Gah? To destroy Kona would require you to banish Kola also, for Kola could no longer hold his head up with pride within the Tor-Gah, such would be the shame of Kona's death at your jaws.' Torkahn remained silent as he watched the elder Sirion with one keen eye. He had already asked himself all of these same questions many times. Taking care to meet Sirion's eye, Torkahn toned his acceptance of Sirion's concern.

'You have an alternative course of action to suggest?' toned Torkahn, knowing that Sirion would never have asked for this meeting without his first having something in mind.

'I have shared tone with the Tor-Gah-Toh,' toned Sirion, staring toward the huge shadow of the old whale moving slowly in the water ahead.

'The old one has swum for many cycles on his last great journey, Tor. He swims alone to his last dive in the great cold.' Hearing Sirion's tone, Torkahn could feel the chill of that cold sea.

'Kola should be spared the pain of seeing his father defeated,' toned Sirion. 'I would ask, Tor, that you might spare Kona from a certain death, and instead, offer him one last chance to make amends in return for his wasted life. The Tor-Gah-Toh requires safe passage to the cool waters of his ancestors, Tor. Perhaps the old one should have an escort? A bodyguard to ensure that this great traveller reaches his far distant destination in safety?' Listening respectfully Torkahn considered Sirion's proposal. He had heard the echo of truth sounding in Sirion's tone. He did not wish to be forced into a fight to the death with Kona. Not in front of the innocent and highly impressionable Kola. Torkahn had grown to like the young whale. But how could he be sure that Kona would see out this task; this last duty to the Tor-Gah, whom he had so foully betrayed? Sensing that Torkahn was swimming against currents of strong feeling and duty, Sirion bowed his head as he sent his last tone to Torkahn.

'You are concerned that once Kona is out of your sight, then he will abandon his duty?' called Sirion. 'You have my word, Tor, that should Kona even think of leaving the company of our old friend here, then I shall hear of it,' toned Sirion.

'I have no doubt of it,' returned Torkahn. 'Very well, Sirion, I shall swim to your course as you request. 'Thank you, Tor. You do me honour,' returned Sirion.

Kona knew that he was beaten even before he had begun. To stand and fight Torkahn now would be foolish. Although he was confident that he could give a good account of himself if required, he was also concerned that even if he was fortunate enough to beat Torkahn in an epic battle of strength against strength, that he could be left with injuries that could hamper his cold and cunning plot. He knew that this was neither the time nor the place for mock heroics. He shifted his gaze toward the shadowed forms of Kato and Daks. Neither whale would meet his eye. He could sense that they would like to tear him fin from fin, now that they so obviously knew the truth, and the true depth of his treachery. Kona swam on his guard. Aware that the only thing preventing the others from attacking him was the Tor's hardened tone, and the distant shape of the silently swimming Kola. His only son.

Kona watched as Torkahn's shadow emerged from the darkened pre-dawn gloom. He could feel Torkahn's eyes studying him with a renewed interest. Closing his eyes Kona prepared himself for what was to come.

Torkahn swam to confront Kona nose to nose. With Torkahn's return, Kato and Daks moved quietly aside, their forms causing hardly a ripple on the darkened sea.

Torkahn swam slowly in a tight circle around Kona as if he was preparing to fight. Kona attempted to follow Torkahn with his eyes, but he soon found that he was feeling dizzy and disoriented. Wondering how long he would have to wait before Torkahn made his move, Kona jumped in the sea as Torkahn's tone echoed through the short space of sea between them.
  'I will not challenge you, Kona, as is my right,' toned Torkahn. 'But know this Koh-neh-nah, that you would surely die this day had not your own son been present to witness your disgrace. I will not punish Kola further by forcing him to bare witness to his own father's well deserved demise.'

Torkahn floated rigidly in the water, his jaw hanging open to display his fearsome array of teeth, his forced silence hanging in the sea, as if daring Kona to make just one wrong move. Kona was finished.
  'You are instead banished to the furthest reaches of the blue,' toned Torkahn.

'In return for my sparing you your life, Kona, I offer you the opportunity to make amends in the eyes of your son, Kola. You will swim with and offer aid to the whale Ko-luk-tou, who even now awaits your arrival. You will accompany Ko-luk-tou on his long journey to the south, Kona. And do not think that you can abandon your duty to me or to the very sea itself, as I will hear of it as surely as mighty Rah rises each dawning.

You will never darken my waters again, Kona,' toned Torkahn, in a way that made Kona's head hang even lower in the sea. Kona made neither sound nor movement as he listened to Torkahn's sentence, but behind his dull, dark eye, he knew now that he was beaten. He felt Torkahn's final tone enter his ear like the barbed tail of a flat-head.

'As for your son, Kola, he will remain with me, swimming under my care and protection.
Unlike you, Kola will continue to occupy his rightful place as a valued member of the Tor-Gah.'

Kona did not know whether to vent or to breathe. He had a simple choice, either play babysitter to an ageing relic, or risk death in a fight to the finish with Torkahn. Even if he managed to somehow defeat Torkahn, Kona knew that he would have to fight every bull in the pod to finally win control. That he would also never see his son again hung like a weight of rocks around his tail.

Dropping head in defeat, Kona accepted his fate. 'I hear you, Tor.'

Torkahn floated in silence, the sea the only sound that dared to break the tone of his next call. 'So be it then. It is done.'

17.

A new trust and a new beginning.

With Kona finally dealt with, it was not long before the whale known as Ko-luk-tou was at last out of sight, swimming south, his smaller escort now invisible to a son who had had to farewell his father for the last time.

A saddened Kola swam silently in company with Torryn and Sirion, as together they followed in Torkahn's wake, on the return swim to locate Rally, and the by now, anxiously awaiting members of the pod.

'We'll soon be back swimming with mother and Nee-Lah again,' called Torryn happily.

'You will like Nee-Lah, Sirion. She has travelled many tides and she can remember stories going back over ninety summers.'

'I shall look forward to hearing Nee-Lah's tales,' toned Sirion. Angling his head, Sirion tensed in the sea as if he had sensed something.

'You must answer to your father's call, Torryn,'

he called. Swimming with his mind on other things, Torryn had not heard his father's tone calling for him. Before he could share his next tone he heard his father's unique call reaching through the sea to find his ear.

'How did you know?' toned Torryn, looking at Sirion with ever increasing wonder.

'My life, is your life, Torryn,' returned Sirion. 'Now swim quickly to your father. And remember, Torryn, you must always answer to his call before my own.'

Torryn looked into Sirion's eye and he understood. Torkahn was his father and the Tor. Torryn knew that his first loyalty must always be to his father and to the other members of his pod. Leaving Sirion and Kola, he moved quickly through the sea before locating Torkahn swimming alone well ahead of Kato and Daks.

'I am here, father,' he called.

On hearing his youngest son's call, Torkahn thanked the spirits of the deep for Torryn's safe return. 'I see you, Torryn. Swim with me, Torryn-Gah. I wish to share tone with you about what has happened here today,' toned Torkahn.

'I must apologise to you, Torryn. That Kona chose to take out his anger against me by risking your life is partly my own fault.' Swimming at his father's side Torryn swam unsure if he should reply or not.

'This was none of your doing, boy. Kona was weak and he envied the trust and confidence that I share with you and your brothers. Had he only thought of his own son more, then Kona may have chosen to swim to a different course,' toned Torkahn. 'Kona placed your life in danger, Torryn. He can swim grateful that I spared him his miserable life.' Although he didn't really understand his father's meaning, Torryn's only thoughts were for his friend, Kola. Alone now, without his own father or mother.

'And Kola, father? What will happen to him? He is alone now,' piped Torryn. Torkahn swam pleased that Torryn's thoughts were for Kola.

'Kola will have to learn to forget, Torryn. He has his place here, at my side, where I can keep an eye on his progress, and where Sirion can see to his education. I promised Kola that his father's actions would never reflect badly upon him in my eyes, Torryn. He is one of us. We must build on that bond of trust,' toned Torkahn. Torryn thought about this.

'I will do my best to see that Kola is never left out, father. I will never forget how he toned against his father for me.'

'You acted well, my son. As I would expect from you. You kept your senses about you when many others with your short time in the sea would have been lost. The sea has delivered you back safely to us. For that we must all be thankful.'

'It was Sirion who saved me, father,' toned Torryn. '

'Yes, Sirion.....,' returned Torkahn with some deep thought..

'Don't you like Sirion, father?'

'It is not a matter of liking Sirion, Torryn. It is a matter of respect. I owe Sirion a great debt of thanks for his returning you safely to us. My only concern is that you are happy to swim with Sirion, and for you to learn all that he has to share with you. It is a lot to ask of a whale who enjoys the freedom of the wide open spaces of the sea,' toned Torkahn.

Swimming at his father's side Torryn considered his tone. It was most certainly true that many strange things had happened since the mysterious Sirion had first rescued him from certain death from the embrace of the deadly kelp. He listened as Torkahn continued.

'You will have to learn to understand things that seem very strange to you, Torryn. I wish to prepare you for this life that Sirion offers you. The choice is yours and yours alone to make, Torryn-Gah.' Torryn remained calm. He enjoyed it when his father shared tone with him in this way.

'I will have powers, father?' he toned.

'Yes, Torryn. With such power also comes great responsibility.'

Torryn met his father's eye. 'I understand, father. I shall do my best for you and mother.'
'That is well, Torryn. And please know that we are both very proud of you,' returned Torkahn.

As the sun reached its highest point in a blue, cloudless sky, a single tone echoed throughout the small pod of returning whales.
'I see you, Tor,' sounded the familiar tone of Rally's musical greeting, carried across a great distance to the sharp senses of his father. After a few short breaths, Torkahn, Torryn, Daks and Kato were bathing in the welcoming echoes and reassuring tones of the pod. Swimming at Sirion's side, Kola, too, felt the welcoming sounds of those they had left behind.

Swimming in the van of the greatly reduced pod was Sorryl. Torkahn could see her regal head pushing quickly through the sea as she swam strongly with Rally at her side.
Sorryl had taken to swimming with Rally each day, using her far reaching senses to search the sea in vain for any sign of her only son. With his snout placed just ahead of Sorryl's, Rally swam with Soh-nee and Sey-la swimming on each flank. With the ever vigilant Nee-Lah swimming in the centre of the small group, her smiling eyes placed firmly on both Torney and Nayla, who swam obediently at her side, and who were for once, both strangely silent.

Sirion's great bulk caused quite a stir, not the least with Nee-Lah, who could be heard pining high above the rest for the joyful return of those she had missed the most. Surfing through the waves, Sorryl swam to greet Torryn. Her joy at finding her son alive and well and returned to her unharmed, was the answer to all her calls to the sea. Torryn wriggled and squirmed in the sea as Sorryl pressed herself as close as she could to her only son.

Nuzzling and singing in celebration of his return, Sorryl fussed and crooned until Torryn, who really deeply appreciated his mother's doting attention, did his best to swim free, his ears echoing to the added and much welcomed teasing tones of Torney and Nayla.

Escaping Sorryl's attentions, Torryn swam to meet the twins who immediately began squirming and nuzzling him with their snouts, just as Sorryl had done. Torryn never imagined that he would be so relieved to hear their silly taunts and calls as he was right at that moment. Enjoying the close contact of those he had missed the most, he realized within himself that he had somehow changed. Torney and Nayla, too, could sense that there was indeed something very different about the newly returned Torryn.

Nee-Lah floated happily enjoying the sights and sounds of this noisy family reunion. She too had recognized the change in Torryn. He was growing up. With Sirion to swim with him and to guide him, Nee-Lah swam happy that the spirits and currents of the blue had made the right choice, and returned Torryn to his rightful place. For Nee-Lah, Sirion's arrival was an added and a most pleasing blessing. That the mighty Sirion was also a fine figure of a whale also added much to Nee-Lah's eye.

After all the greetings and joyful messages of reunion had been completed, Torkahn toned for silence. Even the boisterous Torney and Nayla ceased their endless pining as Torkahn toned to the pod for silence. 'I see you members of the Tor-Gah,' he toned, who along with Torryn, swam slowly alongside the impressive form of Sirion.

'May I present Sirion, friend to the Tor-Gah and saviour of Torryn. This trusted bull has shown true and loyal service to myself, and through me, to you, the pod Tor-Gah,' toned a very grateful Torkahn. 'If Sirion would wish it, I invite him to become a member of the Tor-Gah as of this day, with all the privileges and bounties that are due to him as a mentor to my son, and as a valued member of my van,' toned Torkahn, his echo sounding his own relief at Torryn's safe return.

Sirion swam pleased. He was more than aware that his presence might be seen by others to be a challenge to the Tor in itself. But Sirion had stated his desire to swim with the Tor-Gah so that he might be permitted to continue to educate Torryn in the hidden ways of the chosen. Sensing that Sirion's only thought was for the safety and future security of his youngest son, Torkahn and Sorryl were both more than pleased to repay the old bull's kindness to their son. If Sirion was hoping to swim in peace in his advancing years, then Torkahn knew that Sirion had better be prepared for a life filled with the demands of his youngest and his most adventurous son's continuing education.

Meeting Sorryl's eye through the throng of toning, splashing whales, Torkahn could sense her true happiness. Sorryl could swim safely assured that Torryn would always be swimming under Sirion's all-seeing eye. Their son had been returned to them by the hidden currents of the blue. For this blessing they were both truly thankful.

The surrounding Orca, as was their habit in such a happy situation, slapped their tails on the surface of the sea in a shower of foam and spray, a sure sign of their shared pleasure and acceptance of Sirion into their daily lives.
Bowing his noble head, Sirion sent his short tone

of appreciation ringing out through the sea.

'I hear you, Tor.'

Daks floated quietly next to Rally as he watched Sirion closely.

'We have much to thank Sirion for,' toned Rally.

'We do?' returned Daks.

'Sirion tells me that I too have such abilities sleeping within me,' toned Rally, self importantly. Daks nudged his brother.

'The only part of you that does not sleep is your stomach, brother,' toned Daks.

Rally chose to ignore Daks' teasing tone.

'You are a chosen one, Rally,' toned Daks. 'Chosen to swim the next patrol!'

Rally moved off to share tales of his own greatness with his mate, leaving Daks to float alone. Daks swam quietly as he watched the tall sailed Sirion who swam with young Kola close to his side.

'Thank you, Daks.' Sirion's silently delivered message made Daks jump in the sea. He knew then that Torryn's new friend was going to take quite some getting used too!

The story of Torryn's adventures travelled quickly throughout the pod. The news of Kona's planned treachery surprising few who heard it.

Torkahn saw to it that Kola took the place of his father, swimming in his position on the pods seaward flank.

A position of great trust, and a sign to the pod that Kola had earned the Tor's trust and respect, and that Kola should remain a trusted and much valued member of the pod.

Together with Torryn's friendship, and an ever watchful Sirion's firm guidance, Torkahn swam confident that Kola would soon return to being a happy and productive member of his adopted family.

Searching for Torryn at her side, Sorryl found that he had again managed to slip away through the crowded sea. Torryn swam in search of one whale. 'I see you, Kola,' he called, catching sight of Kola swimming alone on the outskirts of the pod. Torryn swam to his friend's side.

'It is so good to have you back, Torryn-Gah,' toned Kola shyly.

'It is good to be back,' agreed Torryn. 'I had to thank you for your tone in my defence, Kola,' toned Torryn, trying hard not to mention Kona's name. 'If it was not for you, anything could have happened.'

'I only did what I could, Torryn. I did what your father the Tor would expect me to do,' toned Kola. 'You are my friend, Kola. We have shared a lot together. We must make sure that we always swim close from now on, so that no whale will ever be able to swim between us,' called Torryn. 'From today we all swim as one.'

Kola looked Torryn in the eye and was glad that Torryn was the whale that he was.

'Join me swimming next to Sirion, Kola. He has stories to share that would scare Nee-Lah white!' toned Torryn excitedly. Kola winked his eye and swam to follow Torryn. He had no understanding as to why his father had acted as he had. But he knew now how fortunate he was to have a friend like Torryn and his place within the Tor-Gah.

As the days turned into weeks, and the weeks into months, the reunited family made steady progress through the warming blue water of the coastal waterways. Food was plentiful and Torkahn swam pleased with the distance they had covered, and the amount of seaway they had put behind them, as he led the pod to claim the tasty rewards of another successful mornings hunt. Unnoticed by Rally, Kato and the other bulls of the van, Torkahn angled his head slightly to peer back and behind himself to the rear most position of his sprawling pod.

There, as they always seemed to be now, swam the familiar sight of Sirion's great sail stretching high into the brilliant blue of a clear spring sky.

Swimming next to him was the smaller, but just as grand sight of Torryn's sail, slowly rising and falling in rhythm to the cradling swell of the sea. All seemed to be well to Torkahn's eye.

They had made good progress through the gently slopping waves. The pod swam on, the touch of the welcoming rays of Rah warming each of their shining backs. Torkahn enjoyed listening to the echoing tones of the pod as they flooded the sea with their musical pleasure at the promise of the next hunt, a full belly, and of the bright new day that lay ahead.

Moving through a sparkling sea Torryn swam close to his new friend's solid flank. He knew that he had been very lucky to survive Zaar's ferocious attack. He owed Sirion a great deal for having saved his life. Making a silent promise to himself that he would do his utmost to never disappoint Sirion, or let him down in any way, Torryn felt the scar on his back give its own familiar twinge. His imagination swam through the sea in search of cold-bloods. The three rules of survival ran through his mind as he scanned the sea around him.
Where you see no eyes, there are eyes upon you.
Where you see no life, there hides a multitude.
Where you sense no danger, there danger lurks!

Swimming not far away, and having already forgotten his latest tangle with the black and white Orca, Zaar, having survived to live another day, swam alone, his senses scanning the sea for his next easy meal, his nose seeking that next tantilising scent of freshly spilled blood.

The End.

Join Torryn and the pod Tor-Gah as they swim
beneath a new moon and the
flooding of a new tide, in Torryn's next adventure,
"When World's Collide."